SIDEKICKS CHALLENGER

21 LIFE-CHANGING CHALLENGES TO EMPOWER TEENS

SIDEKICKS CHALLENGER

21 LIFE-CHANGING CHALLENGES TO EMPOWER TEENS

A COMPANION TO *SIDEKICKS: HELPING YOUTH SUCCEED AGAINST THE ODDS*

REED THOMAS
WITH NADINE MATIS, PhD

Copyright © 2018 by Reed Thomas

All rights reserved, including the right to reproduce this book, or portions thereof, in any form. No part of this book may be used or reproduced in any manner whatsoever without written permission from the author, except in the case of brief quotations embodied in critical articles and reviews. The views expressed herein are the responsibility of the author and do not necessarily represent the position of the publisher. For information or permission, write: rthomas@reedthomas.org.

This is a work of creative nonfiction. The events herein are portrayed to the best of the author's memory. While all the stories in this book are true, some names and identifying details may have been changed to protect the privacy of the people involved.

Editorial work and production management by Eschler Editing
Cover design by Kimberly Kay Durtschi
Interior print design and layout by Kimberly Kay Durtschi
eBook design and layout by Eugene Woodbury

Published by Scrivener Books

First Edition: November 2018
Printed in the United States of America

ISBN 978-1-949165-05-0

To the SideKicks, for lessons learned

CONTENTS

Foreword .... *i*
Introduction .... *iii*
How to Use This Book .... *v*
Chapter One—The Duskee Story *1*
Chapter Two—Impressions *7*
Chapter Three—Choices *13*
Chapter Four—Sixth Sense *19*
Chapter Five—Judging Wisely *27*
Chapter Six—Persistence *35*
Chapter Seven—Fun *43*
Chapter Eight—Unique Gifts and Talents *47*
Chapter Nine—Opportunity *53*
Chapter Ten—The Power of Goals *59*
Chapter Eleven—Natural Highs *67*
Chapter Twelve—Activities *73*
Chapter Thirteen—Role Models and Mentors *79*
Chapter Fourteen—Giving and Receiving *85*
Chapter Fifteen—Innovations *91*
Chapter Sixteen—Things Are Hard before They Are Easy *97*
Chapter Seventeen—Stay the Course *103*
Chapter Eighteen—Steer Your Mind *109*
Chapter Nineteen—Visualize Success *113*
Chapter Twenty—Resilience *119*
Chapter Twenty-One—Affirmations *125*
Chapter Twenty-Two—A Twenty-One-Year Challenge *131*
Chapter Twenty-Three—Your Life Story *135*
Chapter Twenty-Four—Golden Reconnections *139*
Promptings *143*
Acknowledgments *153*
About the Authors *155*
Note to Readers *157*
Endnotes *159*

FOREWORD

I was very happy when I read *SideKicks* by Reed Thomas because I knew it would be a great help to administrators, school counselors, and teachers in any high school.

With his SideKicks program, Reed found a way to motivate the students he worked with and help them believe in themselves and their dreams. This helped many to graduate and excel in their lives. This new book is a wonderful sequel to *SideKicks*. In it Reed seeks to empower any teenager to become part of the next Greatest Generation. Reed presents twenty-one life-changing challenges that if accepted and implemented, will set any teen on a path toward success.

—*Nadine Matis, PhD*

INTRODUCTION

Four decades ago, an innovative rodeo program was introduced at North Sanpete High School. That program sparked an interest among previously disengaged students and led to changed lives. As those students became active participants, they experienced natural highs and a camaraderie that has followed them throughout their lives.

Depending on location and circumstance, rodeo certainly will not be the answer for everyone. Different locales and cultures support varying traditions and interests. Nevertheless, with dedication and commitment, the underlying lessons learned by the original SideKicks participants can be applied in a wide variety of settings and circumstances, as the principles are universal in nature.

Rodeo superstars Mickey Young, Don Gay, and Gary Leffew left their impact as mentors for the students of North San Pete High. The book *Psycho-Cybernetics*[1] by Dr. Maxwell Maltz, which Gary Leffew introduced to these students, became an important source of motivation for them. From that source came the idea for the twenty-one-day challenge presented in this sequel. Dr. Maltz found that it typically takes twenty-one days to solidify a habit.

In this new book, the SideKicks adventure becomes a jumping-off point for life-changing lessons that can be used by students as well as parents, students, educators, school administrators, and others. Though not every reader will get the same message, all will come out empowered to create a life of meaning and success.

Recently I was approached by a man I didn't recognize. When he said, "I want to thank you for saving my life," I was intrigued. It turned out that some of the positive concepts he had gotten from a class I'd taught forty years ago had kept him from taking his own life during a difficult period.

That is really what got me thinking more about writing this sequel. The concepts introduced here are often left out of school curriculums. Yet the need for them has never been greater. High school dropouts, youth suicides, bullying, drug abuse, self-esteem problems, and a host of related issues continue to escalate among our teens.

The lessons to be learned from the SideKicks will empower young people as they move into a position to become the next greatest generation. And the lessons learned will also be a valuable tool for adult mentors and role models as well.

While part of the SideKicks experience is my story, this book is not about me. It is not about the SideKicks. It is not even about the others mentioned in it. It is about you. By connecting these dots, your dreams, passions, and life purpose can be enhanced. This sequel will empower you to enjoy the kind of lifestyle you want for yourself. And for role models and mentors, it will help you to better connect with them.

—Reed Thomas

HOW TO USE THIS BOOK

This may not be a book you just sit down and read from cover to cover as you would *SideKicks: Helping Youth Succeed against the Odds*. This book calls for action.

We suggest reading the beginning, including the Duskee Story, then browsing through the chapters, reading those that capture your interest. After reading the final chapters, pick a challenge to focus on for twenty-one days. Allow these challenges to be your stepping stones for a better life experience.

Writer, author, and poet Rod Miller states in the closing chapter of this book that his challenges have now become a twenty-one-year challenge and have helped him become a best-selling author. Like Rod, never give up in pursuing your passions and dreams.

Living is a little like writing a book. We craft a book word by word, page by page, chapter by chapter. Our lives follow a similar pattern. Choose and apply the following challenges to empower yourself for a more fulfilled life.

It is recommended that you have an action partner, friend, or someone you trust to support you and listen to you and provide feedback as you create the kind of life you desire.

The Duskee Story, Challenge #1	Date Started_____
Impressions, Challenge #2	Date Started _____
Choices, Challenge #3	Date Started _____
Sixth Sense, Challenge #4	Date Started _____
Judging Wisely, Challenge #5	Date Started _____
Persistence, Challenge #6	Date Started _____
Fun, Challenge #7	Date Started _____
Unique Gifts and Talents, Challenge #8	Date Started _____
Opportunity, Challenge #9	Date Started _____
The Power of Goals, Challenge #10	Date Started _____

Natural Highs, Challenge #11   Date Started _____
Activities, Challenge #12   Date Started _____
Role Model/Mentor, Challenge #13   Date Started _____
Giving and Receiving, Challenge #14   Date Started _____
Innovation, Challenge #15   Date Started _____
Things Are Hard before
    They Are Easy, Challenge #16   Date Started _____
Stay the Course, Challenge #17   Date Started _____
Steer Your Mind, Challenge #18   Date Started _____
Visualize Success, Challenge #19   Date Started _____
Resilience, Challenge #20   Date Started _____
Affirmations, Challenge #21   Date Started _____

CHAPTER ONE

The Duskee Story

Early one morning in 1930, J. Leo Seeley climbed into his nearly new Model-A Ford truck at his home in Mount Pleasant, Utah, and headed south down highway 89 to Arizona to purchase some sheep for his ranch. On arrival, Leo met a Navajo Indian boy he guessed to be about eight, maybe ten years old. The boy didn't know his age because he had never attended school.

This boy was herding a small band of sheep alone on the reservation. He seemed forgotten and looked unkempt. Mr. Seeley was concerned, especially when he looked into eyes that seemed filled with sadness. The boy told Mr. Seely his name was Duskee and that his mother had died and his father had given him away for a sack of flour. For a man as kind-hearted as Mr. Seeley, this must have hit a sore spot. He had children of his own at home, and five years earlier he had lost his fourteen-year-old son, Robert, to a tragic work accident. Suddenly he had a choice to make.

Duskee must have been in awe as he climbed into Mr. Seeley's truck. It might have been his first experience sitting inside an auto. They headed to the Indian Agency headquarters in Tuba City.

They located Duskee's father and learned that Duskee's mother had indeed passed away. The father said he could not take care of Duskee alone and didn't really want the child. Desperate times sometimes make people say things they otherwise wouldn't, but no matter the reason, it must have cut the boy deep.

Mr. Seeley couldn't just walk away from the young boy. That would haunt him for the rest of his life. But would his wife and children accept a stranger moving in with them? He continued to wrestle with these thoughts as a person at the agency helped get Duskee cleaned up and new clothes to wear.

Mr. Seeley had come to purchase sheep. He ended up with a small Indian boy as a passenger. Arriving home late in the evening, Mr. Seeley noticed the lights in his house were out. His family had gone to bed. He decided the best place for Duskee to sleep through the night was in his auto. Then, the next morning, well, he would see what the outcome was. This being the beginning of the Great Depression, little did Mr. Seeley realize the financial struggle he would face with so many mouths to feed in his household. Nor did Duskee know what his future held, just that he was far from any home he had ever known.

Early the next morning, Mrs. Seeley raised the blinds of her bedroom window to get some sunshine. As she looked out the window, she saw a small Indian boy standing on the side of their automobile looking lost and alone, a worried expression on his face.

As her husband shared the story with the family, it melted their hearts. As they gathered together at the breakfast table, the discussion was centered on that little boy. He had to have a home; even the children agreed to accept him as a member of their family.

He was invited in and given breakfast. They invited him to take a bath. New clothes were purchased for him. They showed him around the home place, gave him a job to be responsible for just like the rest of the children, and continued to reassure him he was finally home. After three weeks, Duskee began to feel comfortable in his new home and with his new adopted family. That twenty-one-day thing began to work for him.

As it did, he became a devoted, loyal son and brother for the next fourteen years. He worked hard and enjoyed taking care of the livestock. He was given his own pony to ride and studied hard in school.

Charlie McKay, longtime resident of Mount Pleasant, recalled one time when he was visiting the Seeleys by their corral. Mr. Seeley and Duskee had a colt snubbed up to a post in the center of the pen. Charlie watched as they placed the saddle on the back of that unbroke horse. When all was ready, Duskee climbed into the saddle, and Mr. Seeley untied the rope from the post. Charlie said, "That horse really bucked as it went around and around. Duskee managed to stay on until it quit bucking. Then Duskee told Mr. Seeley to open the gate, and he rode the horse through it and down the road, heading south. Mr. Seeley said, "By the time he gets to the ranch, that horse will be broke."

Twelve miles down the road was a section of ground in the middle of irrigated grassland homesteaded by his father. This 640-acre parcel of land, or the ranch, was a dream come true for Duskee. He spent many a day with Mr. Seeley and his adopted brothers doing ranch work there. He enjoyed the freedom of being outdoors—something he connected with from his time spent on the reservation.

Charlie recalls a few memories of Duskee: "Duskee was a little older than his classmates, but no one really knew his correct age. He enjoyed athletics and excelled in track. During the winter when the snow was deep, he could be seen running around the football field. His coach, Mr. Brunger, told me he was the fastest trackman on the team. Duskee also enjoyed the cowboy life he had learned from the Seeleys. He was rarely without his black cowboy hat and usually rode his spotted pony to school, often with one of his adoptive brothers hitching a ride.

"One of Duskee's adoptive brothers was about his age and had a reputation for enjoying a good fistfight. On one occasion someone said to him, "Why don't you take on Duskee?" He replied, "Oh no. He is my brother." The truth being he knew he couldn't beat Duskee in a fistfight."

At school, Duskee studied hard. He also became an all-star athlete. He played the trombone in the marching band while being a member of the varsity football team. He had many friends. At the school dances, all the girls wanted to dance with him. When Duskee graduated from North Sanpete High, he graduated with honors. His future looked bright. Maybe he would even become a valuable contributor among his people on the reservation someday.

After graduation, Duskee was helping to break a colt in Nephi, thirty miles west of Mount Pleasant, when it kicked him. At first he seemed not to be hurt too bad, but his health continued to decline. A family friend, Dr. Madsen, along with Mr. Seeley and his wife, traveled with Duskee back to the Navajo Indian reservation in Arizona. They hoped a doctor from among his own people could better help him get well, but not long afterward, Duskee died in that Arizona hospital of leukemia. He is buried in Tuba City.

"Would they have preferred to bury him in the Mount Pleasant cemetery with his adoptive parents?" Charlie McKay asked. "Yes, but back then, the Indians did not embalm their dead, therefore Duskee had a hurried burial. Duskee was always proud of his Indian heritage, and his remains being buried among his people gave the Seeley family some comfort, even though Leo always felt a sting of regret that Duskee wasn't buried closer to the family who loved him so deeply."

Duskee's story teaches us that great joy comes from reaching out with open hearts and arms to others, even those outside our comfortable circle of family and friends. Family is who we choose to love and serve. Caring for others must always take priority over what's comfortable and convenient. And there's another lesson to be learned from this story.

Duskee lived with the Seeleys for fourteen years. Most of those years were during the Great Depression. Times were tough. The Seeleys even came close to their ranch being repossessed. A friend, Royal Allred, reached out and helped them save their ranch. On the entrance to their ranch was a sign that read, "In appreciate to Royal Allred." That sign hung from that gatepost for years. The kindness Mr. Seeley had given to Duskee came back to him through a friend, proving that when we send good out into the world, it always comes back to us, though oftentimes in unexpected ways.

Duskee was legally adopted by the Seeley family. Until he died, he was proud of his last name being Seeley, and they remained proud of him. This was evident the day I drove to the Mount Pleasant cemetery and located their burial plot. J. Leo Seeley passed away in 1971. His wife followed him four years later. On her tombstone are the names of their eight children, including Duskee. Today, Mr. and Mrs. Seeley, along with their children, have all passed away. However, Duskee's story continues to live on in the hearts of those who hear it.

My thoughts: Helping youth succeed, especially against the odds, can be challenging at first, as it was for the Seeley family, no doubt. However, there is no greater feeling than when one's efforts allow another to become a better person and to find success, acceptance, and genuine happiness.

Comments from Nadine: My personal thought from this beautiful story is that we can't reach out to help another person without helping ourselves. When we help others, our own spirit grows. We become "more," even as they do.

Your thoughts?

Your 21-Day Challenge

A 21-day challenge could be to look for others in your school who are struggling and offer them an act of kindness.

_____
_____
_____
_____
_____
_____
_____
_____
_____
_____
_____
_____
_____
_____
_____
_____
_____
_____
_____
_____
_____
_____
_____
_____

CHAPTER TWO

Impressions

It never ceases to amaze me the power of impressions and the impact they have on our lives. Those impressions, good or bad, are often dependent on our choices.

In the living room in my home sits my old school desk with my initials carved on it. That desk once sat in the old county schoolhouse built in 1903. That tells me this particular desk is well over a century old. My father may have also sat at this very desk as a student. I remember it being desk number three in the sixth-grade row of five desks. I even recall carving my initials in it, and a horse head, indicating my love for horses even back then. That desk leaves behind some deep impressions.

In that desk I recall reading *Smoky the Cowhorse*[2] by Will James. The book, written in 1926, tells the story of a difficult horse. Through the intervention of a caring cowhand, Smoky becomes a good horse. In fact, he becomes the best horse in the herd. That book left an impression that has stayed with me for over six decades.

Years later, I accepted an invitation to be employed with the North Sanpete School District. I was assigned to implement the National Dropout Recovery and Prevention Program of 1975 at North Sanpete High School, my alma mater.

Remembering *Smoky the Cowhorse* and its message, I saw these students, considered difficult by some teachers, as having great potential. With Duskee's story also stored in my memory, I saw previously failing students graduating with their diplomas in hand. With high school rodeo as a vehicle, the story of the SideKicks had its beginning. (You can read about the individual students and their adventures with the SideKicks high school rodeo program in *SideKicks: Helping Youth Succeed against the Odds.*)

My thoughts: The stories I've shared so far all have a common thread. In each case, the main characters thought they had run out of hope and options. In reality, they were at the beginning of a new story. Of course, each person (or horse) had to make the choice to accept the new chances life was offering them.

Whatever your story is, you can create a new beginning and take your life in a new direction. And what better time to start than right now? After all, today is the first day of the rest of your life. As you start on your new adventure, I challenge you to take courage from the success stories of others. Everyone, sooner or later, faces their own tough times. But there are thousands of stories of those who fought life's hard battles and won. Each story is a testament that they succeeded and a promise that you can, too. When life brings such a story into your life, accept it as a gift of encouragement. And at the same time that you allow positive stories to influence you in amazing directions, think about the impact impressions have on our lives. Think about the fact that your life is a story and that every day you leave an impression on others. Your words and actions influence others. You can choose to make it a powerful and positive impression that helps another on their life's journey.

Comments from Nadine: I have spent many of the last twenty years helping young people successfully complete missions for The Church of Jesus Christ of Latter-day Saints. These amazing young people volunteer to spend eighteen to twenty-four months far from home to teach spiritual principles and provide practical service around the globe.

Two of those twenty years were spent with my husband as missionaries in Auckland, New Zealand. My assignment was to work with the six mission presidents in the area helping missionaries struggling with personal problems, like homesickness or feelings of depression.

Sometimes "talk therapy" was all that was needed. Other times, I worked with the area physician to help them get on medications that could alleviate their feelings of depression.

But my most successful tool was to get those missionaries to reach out to help another missionary who was also struggling. Sometimes when they began encouraging another missionary to hang in there, not to give up and go home, a struggling missionary would begin listening to their own advice, often serving and completing a very successful mission.

I always encouraged any missionary I worked with to become a role model for other missionaries. I firmly believe this is an important and ongoing endeavor for all

of us, whether we are presently serving formal missions or not. We often don't realize how much influence for good we can have in the lives of others.

Today I continue to work with missionaries and others who are referred to me. I have noticed that as I help them to have happier lives, I feel happier myself. I believe this is a spiritual truth that continues beyond this mortal life.

Your thoughts?

Your 21-Day Challenge

A 21-day challenge may be to leave a good impression when you first meet others.

CHAPTER THREE
Choices

I never cease to be amazed at the great variety of choices life presents us with. Often, many of these choices are made under the influence of our peers. Other choices can grow out of a reaction to our circumstances, our environment, our home life, our past experiences, our emotions, our health, or any number of other events. We could continue with the many reasons we choose what we do, but the bottom line is that our choices, for the most part, are under our control. We are the ones who are really in charge of our life.

I was born in the room my father was, the very same room he passed away in at age eighty-six. My first eight years of education were in a two-room schoolhouse. I contrast that to the time I spent in Manhattan, New York—a radically different environment. Another time I had the opportunity to observe children at a school in Belize, in Central America. In spite of these students' hardships, they were cheerful, optimistic, and dedicated to succeeding at school and in life. It struck me that some of us will make good choices that inspire and uplift, while others will choose self-defeating behaviors no matter their circumstances.

Growing up in my small hometown, my friends were very important in my life. If my friends had wanted to do drugs, I probably would have. They seemed to have had a certain degree of influence over me, and I wanted their acceptance. Now that I have matured, I plainly see how alcohol, drugs, and other bad choices can take away our agency to choose a better life for ourselves. And we often give up our agency to a degree in the choices we make when we are young. Those choices often determine our future.

Studies have shown that young people who consume alcohol and smoke cigarettes at an early age will often end up taking drugs later. I was fortunate that my friends stayed away from drugs, but I get a chill when I realize that had circumstances been different, I may have made choices with devastating consequences.

My thoughts: When I was a teen, age seventy-seven seemed foreign and a lifetime away. Now, as a seventy-seven-year-old looking in my rearview mirror at my teenage years, that generational gap becomes much narrower.

Looking back, my good choices make me proud. The bad ones, well, not so proud. My message to young people is the same as that of world champion bull rider Gary Leffew, which he shared with me in what he wrote on a photo of him riding a bull: "*Always remember, you are the captain of your ship, the master of your destiny.*"

We are our own driver and navigator as we journey through life. We are at the controls. The choices we make along the way are ours. We need to accept complete responsibility for our choices and even how our choices affect others as we connect with them. Playing the "blame game" only gives us an excuse to not help ourselves with our own problems. And there is no turning back the years and starting over. We must continue to live with any problems we create for ourselves.

We all make mistakes. The key is to take those mistakes, learn from them, and then turn the negatives into positives. At my age, if someone tried to steal my agency from me by getting me hooked on drugs, after saying no, I wouldn't just walk away, I would run.

Each unwise action is like a rock we add to the backpack of life. It may be trying a cigarette, or sneaking a drink, or rationalizing that marijuana is no big deal, or other seemingly harmless choices, like not taking schoolwork seriously or not standing up when we see a classmate being treated unkindly. With every poor choice a person makes, the load gets heavier. The good news is that you can stop putting rocks in your pack by making smarter choices. And you can start taking rocks out of your pack by learning from the poor choices you may have made in the past and choosing more wisely. We all make bad choices sometimes. That's a fact of life. But we can all learn from those choices. It isn't always easy, but it is always possible. Lighten your load, because life is so much better without the rocks.

Comments from Nadine: I have a statement taped to my desk lamp in my office. I repeat it whenever I sit down at my desk: "Choice—Not Chance—Determines Destiny."

Like Reed, I believe most of us make a few wrong choices in our life before we learn from those mistakes. Learning from our mistakes, we hopefully begin making better choices that will guide our lives in a better direction.

In my younger years, I spent too much of my babysitting money on name-brand sweaters, skirts, and shoes. These were purchased in my hometown at popular but expensive stores where all the popular kids shopped.

But superseding my wish to be popular was a deep desire to go to college. Finally, I realized that if I was going to fulfill that desire, I had better change my financial situation by choosing less expensive clothes and saving as much of the money I earned as possible.

During my high school years, I concentrated on getting excellent grades. In the summer, most of the money I earned went into my college fund.

I did attend the University of Utah on a full-tuition scholarship, but I still needed to work twenty-five hours a week. Then, as I needed to, I would dip into my college fund to meet the rest of my expenses.

I have sometimes wondered how my life would have been different if I had continued to choose to spend extravagantly on clothes instead of saving.

I have had many years to observe the results of both good and bad choices in the lives of myself, family members, friends, and clients, and I know without doubt that we are always in control of our choices. We must take personal responsibility for our choices and their results. When we make the mistake of blaming others for our life circumstances, we often feel we can't personally change those circumstances. As long as we stay stuck in that false story, life doesn't get better for us. As soon as we understand that we hold the power to change our lives with our choices, we take the first step on an amazing adventure leading to joy and success.

Your thoughts?

Your 21-Day Challenge

A challenge may be to make good choices or start to undo a past choice you regret. Begin by doing this for twenty-one days.

CHAPTER FOUR

Sixth Sense

Merriam Webster defines the sixth sense as "a power of perception like but not one of the five senses; a keen intuitive power."[3]

Mr. Seeley headed to Arizona to purchase sheep and came home with a new son. Often in life, we see patterns and clues that point to guiding forces in our lives that can't be seen but whose effects can be discerned through careful observation and understanding. This certainly seems to be the case with Mr. Seeley's and Duskee's experience. Was it just coincidence that brought them together? I would imagine the entire Seeley family, Duskee included, would say, "Absolutely not!" Many people have experienced the workings of an internal guidance system that leaves them in wonder. Those who have experienced such "coincidences" will tell you there is no such thing as coincidence. Our lives have meaning and purpose, and we have much more help than we can imagine, even if it isn't always obvious.

While in Las Vegas, Nevada, I received an invitation to teach in the very high school I had graduated fifteen years prior. I was told this was a job no one in the school district wanted. Then I was asked if I would be interested in accepting this assignment.

A thought quickly ran through my mind: "Is this offer something I should accept?" I felt squeezed between a rock and a hard place. This decision would have a lasting effect on my family and maybe even many others in ways I couldn't yet see. I was faced with a daunting choice.

I finally decided to rely on my "sixth sense," my inner voice, my gut. I decided I would take it one step at a time and trust that things would work out as they should. I felt I needed to put my trust in my gut feeling, that sixth sense we all feel when things are to be or are not to be.

Depending on our background, culture, or belief system, we may use other names for these feelings, but they all describe a common truth. Some of these names include instinct, heart, Light of Christ, one's intuition and inner voice, an inner feeling, a gut feeling. Whatever you call it, sometimes our inner guidance system may begin with a thought that just seems to pop into our head.

Below is a small selection of quotes that show how powerful truths "pop up" in every culture, land, and time period:

> *"All that we is the result of what we have thought."*
> —Buddha

> *"A man is but a product of his thoughts. What he thinks, he becomes."*
> —Gandhi

> *"Imagination is everything. It is the preview of life's coming attractions."*
> —Albert Einstein

Sometimes it can be difficult to decide if the thoughts and feelings we are experiencing are coming from us or from a higher source. How can we tap into that guiding power in our lives? Here are a few helpful tips to sort it all out:

1) The wrong environment can prevent us from recognizing the promptings of our inner sense. Drugs and drinking, for example, can numb our ability to identify our sixth sense and follow it wisely. Likewise, filling our minds with negativity, whether it be the angry trolling that takes the place of civil conversation in much of social media today, immersion in violent video games or other violent media, or anything that keeps us focused on anger, hatred, or bitterness, can prevent us from hearing the voice that can guide our lives to greater safety and success. Our inner guide functions best when we actively listen to it. We do this by calming our mind and paying attention to our thoughts and feelings, and to do this, it is advisable to find time away from the noise of society. Some

people do that through prayer, others through meditation, and others by communing with nature. The thing all of these have in common? They require that you put down the smartphone; turn off the TV, computer, or radio; take a break from the hectic pace of life, and find a peaceful place to quiet your thoughts and still your mind. Only then will you be likely to recognize the guidance you are looking for.

2) Our inner guide will always lead us to act for the best good of all. It never encourages us to act in ways that violate our agency or the agency of others. It never advocates action that would harm others or trespass upon their constitutional rights. It is always patient, kind, and long-suffering. It always encourages us to treat others with deep respect and civility. It always honors the righteous laws of the land, people's rights, privacy, and property. Any feeling or prompting that breaks these rules is not one that will bring positive results into your life or the lives of those around you. In addition, your true inner guide will always lead to a peaceful, calm, positive feeling. That doesn't mean you never need courage to act on a good prompting. Even good choices can be scary. But you will be able to move forward with confidence that you are doing the right thing.

3) Like all good things in life, learning to recognize inner promptings can take time and practice. But the more you practice, the better you'll get. A word of warning, however: if you ignore your sixth sense when it gives you good advice, it is less likely to come a second time. (That kinda makes sense. If a wise friend gives you good advice and you repeatedly ignore your friend, sooner or later they may stop offering helpful insights.)

My thoughts: "Teddy Roosevelt and his Rough Riders invaded Cuba during the Spanish-American War. The seas were very rough and threatening as the men sailed near the coast in preparation for what would be known as the Battle of San Juan Hill.

The dangerous waters prevented them from anchoring close to the beach, and the lifeboats were their only option. Before climbing into the boats, however, the men pushed the horses and mules overboard, hoping they would instinctively swim toward land. Some of the animals made it. Others, including Teddy Roosevelt's horse, Texas, became confused in the high, churning waters. Losing their sense of direction, they began swimming out to sea. The men, tossed to and fro on the sea, were powerless to save their animals from certain death.

Suddenly, from the distant shore came a piercing sound. A bugler, aware of the seemingly hopeless situation, had lifted his bugle and began to play. He played long and loud, hoping to attract the attention of the ill-fated animals. Recognizing the familiar sound of the bugle and knowing to follow it, many turned, and with all their might, swam toward the clarion call."[4]

The question remains: How important is it for us to trust our gut, to pay attention to our thoughts and to that sixth sense? Can paying attention to those inner feelings help us make better choices and leave a good impression on others? How important is that to you?

Comments from Nadine: I believe we all have a sixth sense. We just need to learn how to "tune in" and then trust it. After I earned my master's degree in counseling, I was offered several jobs. One offer came from Weber State University, where I had done an internship. I was offered a job as an employment counselor. I love being on a campus of any sort and so felt a definite pull in that direction. But the pay was not as good as with the other offers.

Weber County Division of Social Services was also hiring. I had a good friend on the hiring committee and was offered a job that paid more money than the university. While money wasn't my first priority, I did feel strongly that I should find a way to earn enough to make up for what I'd spent on earning the degree.

Next, I was offered a job at the Ogden office of LDS Family Services. I would work facilitating their unwed-mother-and-adoption program. Having known a lot of young unwed mothers over the years, that resonated with me.

Finally, I received a call from a high school principal offering me a position as a counselor at Weber High School. That sounded good, but I would need to drive almost an hour each way to and from work—not what I really wanted.

I decided to make a chart, listing each employment opportunity at the top and under each, writing the positives and negatives. Then I would look at each one and make a logical decision. I considered this a good decision-making tool, one that usually worked for me and had proven helpful to my clients.

After making the chart, I looked my results over carefully. Weber County Social Services seemed the best offer. I felt relieved to have finally made a decision and went to bed.

But I woke up in the middle of the night with a worried feeling. I began wondering if it was related to my employment decision. So I went downstairs to our library where we had a recliner. After saying an earnest prayer, I sat back, lowered the lights, and began to relax and meditate. I was able to get in touch with my subconscious mind or "spirit mind," as I like to call it.

The answer soon came through very clearly. *Take the high school counselor job.* I went back to bed and slept soundly the rest of the night. In the morning, I knew I should listen to my inner voice. I called the high school principal and accepted the position.

What happened after that confirmed that listening to my sixth sense should always take precedence over logic alone. I was only at Weber High for one year, but that year set the stage for the next ten years of my life.

After about a month, I observed that too many average students were falling through the cracks. Lower-achieving students were getting help in the way of special education classes and counselors. And most teachers were only too happy to spend time helping their top students become Sterling Scholars and work toward getting scholarships to their preferred colleges.

I soon learned that many of our average or slightly below average students came from homes where education was not emphasized or other family problems were evident (i.e., divorce, alcohol addiction, etc.). These students weren't getting the help they needed and often skipped school or certain classes on any given day.

I met with the school principal and was given permission to teach a special class for these students. Next, I met with every teacher in the school to identify students who might benefit from such a class. The parents of these students were quite happy to enroll their students in a class if there was a chance it would help them graduate.

I called the class "Understanding Students" because I wanted each one of my students to feel listened to and understood. I loved that class and all those in it. They talked a lot and listened to each other and found they had many problems in common. We laughed and talked and role-played. As I look back, I realize the class really became group therapy.

Every Friday, I stopped by the donut shop on the way to school, and "Donut Friday" soon became tradition. My students had near perfect attendance in my class. Much like Reed's SideKick students, a close camaraderie developed among my students. When one of them lost her father due to an accident, the entire class rallied to her aid and showered her with care and support.

My Understanding Students class gave me the experiences I needed to later develop the Options program for the entire district.

Listening to my sixth sense ended up being a gift for me personally, as well as the hundreds of students who were helped as a result of these two programs.

Your thoughts?

Your 21-Day Challenge

For a 21-day challenge, perhaps you can create a greater connection with your sixth sense when you need to make a decision.

CHAPTER FIVE

Judging Wisely

It is a common human failing that we often judge others hastily, without accurate information and without proper context or compassion. Chances are, pretty much everyone has judged someone unfairly or been judged unfairly themselves. We often hear that we shouldn't judge others, and we all tend to agree. But the problem is more complicated than that.

The fact is, we are continually in a position where we must make judgments. It can actually be wrong to avoid making a judgment call when the situation requires it. For instance, when someone offers us drugs, we hopefully have the common sense to make a judgment that accepting the drug can ruin our lives forever and that the person encouraging us to take the drug doesn't have our best interests in mind. If someone pressures us to do something we feel is wrong, it's smart to be able to judge that we shouldn't follow that advice.

People make wise judgments all the time: No, I won't drink and drive. Yes, I will defend freedom of speech for all, even if some people use it to say things I disagree with. No, I won't hate someone from a group I disagree with. Yes, I will question my commanding officer's orders if I feel they violate the law or the Constitution. No, I won't cheat on that test, even if my peers pressure me to.

And sadly, people make bad judgments all the time. They make judgments about people because of race, culture, religion, political views, gender, background, appearance, financial status, etc.

So we hear that we shouldn't judge when, actually, what we need to do is learn to judge wisely, with kindness but also with reason and patience, being willing to always give the benefit of the doubt and admit that we may not know all the facts, and being open to learning more.

Mr. Seeley could have made a snap judgment about Duskee. However, when he took time to ask the boy a few thoughtful questions, Duskee's answers melted his heart. The result was a whole different outcome for Duskee and the Seeley family. Mr. Seeley could have decided that it wasn't any of his business to get involved and driven on. Looking back from our vantage point, that would not have been the right choice.

Some teachers misjudged some of the students who later became SideKicks. I would hear disparaging comments as I ate my lunch in the faculty lounge:

"We ought to just boot them out."

"Those damn kids were just like this in junior high. I didn't expect them to change."

"Students that can't measure up should be dropped from school and forced into the outside world."

To escape this negativity, I began eating lunch in my classroom, alone. I chose to follow Mark Twain's advice: "Keep away from people who try to belittle ambitions. Small people always do that, but the really great make you feel that you, too, can become great."[5] I also determined to do something positive, and that decision was the start of the SideKicks.

That was 1975. Forty years later, whenever I have an opportunity to reconnect with any former SideKicks, I am filled with great satisfaction at the positive paths they have taken in life. The lessons they learned from SideKicks helped them on their life's journey. Today, they continue to be law-abiding citizens, and the positive effects of their examples continue to ripple outward to benefit their children and grandchildren. The SideKicks' success teaches us be careful how we judge.

Great educator Booker T. Washington once said, "Where ever our lives touch yours, we help or hinder . . . wherever yours touches ours, you make us stronger or weaker. There is no mistake . . . man drags man down or man lifts man up."[6]

A verse in the Bible reads, "Let no corrupt communication proceed out of your mouth, but that which is good to the use of edifying, that it may minister grace unto the heavens" (Ephesians 4:29).

No matter the language or the source, the idea is key to our success in life. When we judge hastily, without giving others the benefit of the doubt, we not only hurt them, we lose touch with our own humanity.

And we cut ourselves off from potential friendships, allies, and fulfilling relationships.

Learning to judge wisely takes a lifetime of practice to perfect. But you can get pretty good results right from the start with a few basic rules:

1) Always give everyone the benefit of the doubt at first.

2) Always assign positive motivations to people's words and actions until you have more information. Even then, give them the benefit of the doubt.

3) Always assume there's more to the person, their words, and their actions, than meets the eye.

4) Always leave room for the idea that your initial impressions may be wrong.

There's a great story that illustrates this point. A man at airport buys a pack of cookies, gets a drink, and settles down to read the paper and wait for his flight. He's surprised when a younger man sits down across from him and even more surprised when a few minutes later, the stranger helps himself to a cookie. The first man takes a cookie and glares at his unwelcome companion, all the while hoping the young man gets the message. But the young man continues to help himself to the older man's cookies, smiling at him each time the older man takes a cookie. Finally, there's one cookie left. The young man breaks it in half and gives part to the older man. The older man can't believe the audacity of the young man. It isn't until he finally boards his plane and opens his carry-on that he sees his own bag of cookies. He was the real cookie thief.

When we keep in mind that we may be wrong, that we may not have all the facts, that we may not understand what someone is dealing with, we open ourselves up to the possibility of true understanding. And that can lead to all sorts of good things.

My thoughts: It felt wonderful to attend a fund-raiser for some qualifiers to the State High School Rodeo Finals. I was among friends, former

SideKicks, students, and their families. It was held in the high school where I had been a teacher for several years before retiring.

The fund-raiser was a success; several items had been donated, and people were generous in their purchases. I was sitting next to an original SideKick and his son. The boy said, "Well, I guess I better go and pay for my purchases." I noticed people standing in a rather long line and said, "Pay for mine, too," and handed him my money.

As I headed out the door, someone yelled, "Reed, you haven't paid!" I called out that I had, but right away came the response from the ladies at the payment table: "No you haven't!"

I began looking for the boy who had taken my money, so he could vouch for me. I couldn't see him anywhere, and I worried that perhaps he had already left the building. Just then, I saw him and signaled to him. He nodded his head, indicating I had paid. One of ladies said, "How did I miss that one?"

I have often thought about that experience. What if my only witnesses had left? What would the outcome have been? Would I have been branded as a liar and a thief among those in attendance? Would that message have spread throughout the community where I live?

My heart went out to those secretaries who I'm sure were as embarrassed as I was. We all make mistakes, and, hopefully, that mistake taught us all a valuable lesson: not to be too hasty until the facts are known. I quickly made up my mind I was not going to allow myself to hold a grudge. I quickly forgave because I'd also made my share of mistakes in the past.

As I run into those two women in a store or elsewhere, we share a friendly smile and kind hello. We are still friends because we turned a negative into a positive. We know, as we go through life, we will all make bad judgment calls, because none of us is perfect.

So, I leave with you a quote by Traci Lea LaRussa: "Judge tenderly, if you must. There is usually a side you have not heard, a story you know nothing about, a battle waged that you are not having to fight."[7]

Comments from Nadine: By judging with kindness, Reed made wise decisions that led to the SideKicks program. When we allow ourselves to be guided by the same kindness and humility, we lift ourselves and everyone around us.

As a therapist, I have sometimes been tempted to feel dismayed at the predicaments my clients are in due to poor choices. But then I remember some of my own poor decisions and I don't feel in any way superior to them. The human factor is in play here. We all make poor choices at times, but hopefully we learn from them and go on to make better choices in the future.

In learning to judge wisely, we must see people as they can become, not as they are now. With this positive attitude, we can work together to help them get where they need and want to be. In the process, we will find that we also are lifted.

At every interview, I always listen to my client first, seeking to understand their needs and desires, and with respect for them and their struggles. I have learned that we cannot help another if we judge them unwisely, or if we feel superior to them. When we learn to see with the heart, when we see all people as our brothers and sisters, deserving of our respect, then we can grow together, lifting them as they lift us.

Your thoughts?

Your 21-Day Challenge

A 21-day challenge may be to not judge another until you have all the facts.

_____
_____
_____
_____
_____
_____
_____
_____
_____
_____
_____
_____
_____
_____
_____
_____
_____
_____
_____
_____
_____
_____
_____
_____

CHAPTER SIX

▲

Persistence

This section may just as easily be called *grit*. I don't mean dirt. I mean the determination required to stick with a decision or goal, even in when faced with difficulty, roadblocks, and opposition.

In 1975, some students at North Sanpete High School wanted to establish a high school rodeo club. Back then, there were no such programs in that area. High school rodeo clubs existed in Utah, but none were connected directly with any high school curriculum. These students wanted a high school rodeo club that was part of their school, and so they circulated a petition.

Jim Thornton, vice principal of the school, approached me one day and explained the situation. Would I consider being their club adviser? The students' persistence created a new chapter at North Sanpete High School and was the beginning of the SideKicks story.

From that point on, this persistence turned into pure grit as the SideKicks made things happen for themselves, learning to ride broncs and bulls. This kind of grit is sometimes called a "cowboy up" kind of persistence. It's when you get bucked off and get right back on. On the internet, we find other examples of persistence taking the spotlight:

Abraham Lincoln failed in business three times and failed campaigning seven times prior to becoming president.

Albert Einstein could not speak until he was three, could not speak fluently until he was nine. His parents felt he was subnormal. He was expelled from school and his teachers described him as "mentally slow."

Michael Jordan was cut from his basketball team for lack of skill.

Bill Gates was a Harvard University dropout. His first business, Traf-O-Data, was a failure.

Thomas Edison's teachers told him he was too stupid to learn anything.

Babe Ruth became one of the greatest hitters in major baseball. He became known as "homerun king" and "king of strikeouts." He struck out 1330 times and hit the most homeruns in 1927, totaling sixty that season.

Elvis Presley was told by the Grand Ole Opry to go back to his truck because he would never go anywhere.

Admiral Robert Peary attempted to reach the North Pole seven times before he made it on try number eight.

In its first twenty-eight attempts to send rockets into space, NASA had twenty failures.

Oscar Hammerstein had five flop shows that lasted less than a total of six weeks before *Oklahoma!*, which ran for 269 days and grossed $7 million.

Oprah Winfrey was fired from an early television reporting job as she told she was not right for TV.

My thoughts: Graduating from high school with a diploma in hand shows grit. Learning a career and staying employed shows grit. Graduating from college shows grit.

Simply stated, being persistent in pursuing one's dreams, goals, and desires demonstrates grit. Becoming a person of great character and integrity demonstrates persistence and grit. Employers often look for that kind of grit in the people they hire. They want to a person who will stay with them through thick and thin. That may be one reason why some look to see if one has a high school diploma, and later a college diploma. That little piece of paper says something about your ability to stick with a tough task all the way to the end.

As I tackled the challenge to write the SideKicks' story, it was grit that brought it to fruition. At first I had to become acquainted with my word-processing software. As I found myself getting into the story, peck by peck, I had a worrisome thought: What if my computer crashed? Asking around, I learned I could save my work onto a flash drive. After growing up with a typewriter, learning my way around a computer was a challenge.

Then there were the dreaded attacks of writer's block. There were times when I felt like trashing the whole manuscript. Instead, I followed the example some of my SideKicks had set for me. Like them, I chose to "cowboy up" when the going got tough.

If those SideKicks had the courage to ride those mean bulls and bronc horses and to get back on again and again after getting bucked off, even stomped on, I should be able to muster the courage to write their story.

Writing is not a natural talent of mine, much like the SideKicks experienced when they first attempted to ride broncs and bulls. However, by being persistent and not giving up, the SideKicks have a story to tell, and I have their story to share, along with the lessons we have learned.

This came to fruition by persistence and not walking away when opportunity knocked.

Comments from Nadine: Persistence means keeping on toward your important goals *no matter what.*

Reed talks about "cowboying up." This is the idea that when you get bucked off the horse, you get right back on. Of course, he is talking about much more than horses here. He means that anytime you are thwarted in reaching your goals, you take the time to reassess what happened and then get right back on your desired path. The historical figures he mentioned are just the tip of the iceberg. Every invention, every good idea, every success, every positive thing that has ever happened in the world has come from someone determined to not give up when the going got tough. Edison is rumored to have tried more than one thousand times before he perfected the light bulb. Almost every book that became a great success was rejected many times at first.

Without men and women who refused to give up, we would not have electricity, computers, planes, antibiotics, organ transplants, vaccines, movies, television, radio, cars, submarines, smartphones, or a million of the other things that make our lives safer, healthier, more exciting, and more interesting. The best thing is, you don't need to be famous to act with grit in your own life. You just need to get back on as soon as life bucks you off your dream.

I'm happy Reed had the grit to finish writing *SideKicks*. I have had ideas for several different books in my life but never followed through. Thankfully, I did show persistence when I began my doctoral program. I was determined I would finish it *no matter what.* One snowy morning, my mother called to say, "You can't drive all the way to Provo today in this bad weather."

I said, "Yes, I can and I will. Don't worry about me. I'll call you when I get home." (That was before the days of cell phones.) I had good tires and drove very carefully to Provo, attended my classes, and later called my mother to tell her I was home and fine. I have never regretted that decision and the others I made under similar circumstances.

But there was one time when I really did almost give up on earning my PhD. I loved my classes and had learned a lot. But near the end of my program, I was faced with writing the doctoral dissertation. The project seemed impossible.

Then I remembered my Understanding Students class and decided I could do research on what would happen if we started a program like that in all three high schools in the district.

We identified students who were in danger of not completing high school and randomly assigned them to two groups. A control group continued their scheduled classes. The other students were enrolled in the Options program.

The only complaints we received were from those parents of the students in the control group. When it became evident during the year that the students in Options were doing better, parents wanted their children removed from the control group and enrolled in Options.

In the following years, there was no control group, as the research was officially over. All students who could benefit from the program were placed in Options. This program continued for several more years in the district.

When the research was finished, I had to write about the results. While I loved the process of research, writing the dissertation itself was tedious.

The temptation to give up or put it off was very real on a daily basis. To overcome this problem, I set a dish of M&M candies by my computer. Whenever I finished a page, I rewarded myself with one candy.

Whenever I got really discouraged, I took a short break to hum "Pomp and Circumstance" while I visualized myself receiving my doctoral robes at commencement. That helped, and I was able to finish.

Winston Churchill is one of my heroes. I remember as a child during World War II hearing him on the radio as he rallied Britain to stand firm against the enemy: "We will fight on the land, we will fight on the seas, we will fight in the air; and we will never, never, never give up."

His persistence and that of countless others is what won the war for the Allies. They had to be persistent to win freedom and defeat tyranny. Your fights will be different but no less important. As long as you never give up, you can reach your goals, your dreams, and create a life of great success and happiness.

Your thoughts?

Your 21-Day Challenge

A 21-day challenge might be to be persistent when opportunity knocks on your door.

CHAPTER SEVEN

Fun

Duskee seemed to find fun whether he was on the dance floor, in team sports, playing a musical instrument, or breaking a horse. He seemed to find enjoyment in whatever he did. Of course, coming from the school of hard knocks, I'm sure he remained ever grateful for what was now his to enjoy. As an educator, I discovered that fun stimulates learning. I have witnessed some great teachers using their gifts and talents to create fun for the students in their classes. One teacher gifted in music used his talents to foster interest and create fun within his classroom. My wife used cartoon drawings in her classes to capture students' interest. Since, I could neither sing, play a musical instrument, nor draw, I used a lariat.

Before and after classes, students would move the desks aside to make room for a roping area. One of my students welded an iron horse in his shop class. He painted it silver and placed a saddle on it. We gave it the name Silver. We also built a dummy calf from an old tire to which we attached three wooden legs. The students called it Sliver, probably because it gave someone a sliver.

Students who previously were late for school started showing up early. I loved the feedback I was getting: "Coming to this class is fun. I love to jump on Silver and rope Sliver." "This contraption makes us want to come to school. It's fun and exciting." "It gives kids a chance to unwind." "This rests my brain from other classes" I've even heard a *yee-haw*! When was the last time you felt that happy?

My thoughts: Our attitude has a huge impact on our ability to learn and grow. And our attitude is totally under our control. Abraham Lincoln said, "Most folks are about as happy as they make up their minds to be."[8]

Some of the happiest people are those who accept challenges and overcome them. They are the ones who live their dreams, passions, and goals. They are usually the ones who end up doing the things that bring them enjoyment, whether it is at their workplace or at play. Some of the unhappiest people are those who avoid challenges. Often, they end up doing the things they don't enjoy doing.

It's important to understand that finding the fun in what you do is different than only doing what you think is fun. Life always requires us to do things that are important and essential for our lives and the lives of others but may not strike us as fun. Changing diapers, unclogging a sink (or worse, a toilet), changing a tire when it's a hundred degrees out or in a blizzard, going through a grueling military training, pulling a twenty-four-hour shift as a medical resident, fighting fires, milking cows at 4:00 a.m., mucking out stables, or going through thousands of lines of code to find a bug in an app are just a few examples.

Every worthwhile job, position, skill, talent, or goal contains a great deal that is "unfun." The secret is to learn to have fun while doing unfun things. Remember why you are doing them and then do the hard, unfun thing with a smile and good cheer.

Successful people learn to have fun no matter what they are doing.

Comments from Nadine: Making learning fun definitely stimulates the whole learning process. In fact, if you can find a way to introduce a little fun even into distasteful activities, they will become easier to do.

When my students looked forward to a variety of donuts every Friday with my class at Weber High, attendance went up because it was more fun. And when I began to reward myself with an M&Ms whenever I wrote a page of my dissertation, the pages were easier to write (and I wrote faster if I was hungry).

In my thirty-seven-year career as a counselor, it has been fun to get to know so many different people well. My work may not strike everyone as fun, but for me, hearing life stories and helping people get their lives back on track is deeply enjoyable (and what better definition of fun is there?)

However, getting on Reed's Silver and roping Sliver would not be fun for me at first glance. But life has taught me that you can find a way to find the fun in any activity. It just takes creativity and a willingness to give it a chance.

Your thoughts?

Your 21-Day Challenge

A 21-day challenge may be to discover joy within in a class you may find challenging or boring by changing your attitude.

CHAPTER EIGHT

▲

Unique Gifts and Talents

A freshman was referred to me by his math teacher. He was failing her math class, and he seemed totally disengaged with school. He wouldn't even try to do his assignments.

I gave him an IQ test and was amazed at the results. He measured way above the norm. I began to wonder why he was performing so far below his potential. He obviously had the smarts, but for some reason, he had put himself in a self-imposed prison. I wondered how many had passed judgment that he was slow or stupid.

We met to discuss his test results. "You have a good head on your shoulders," I said. "I do?" he replied in disbelief. I pointed out the average norm on the graph, then showed him he was far above it. He seemed surprised and became quiet. Then he shared his story with me. "When I was in the third grade, my teacher put me in the lower level in her class. After that, I just gave up trying to learn. I began just watching the time pass on the clock."

Once he saw his test results, he began to see his true potential. During his senior year, he represented North Sanpete High School at the regional math competition at Brigham Young University. He began to develop his unique talent and gift when he had a change of attitude.

I began to wonder how many students in our nation's high schools are disengaged. A quick Google search uncovered a 2003 National Research Council report on motivation, showing that upward of 40 percent of all students are chronically disengaged. But students aren't the only ones dealing with this dilemma. How many teachers today are disengaged when it comes to working with those students? Given a change in attitude, unique gifts and talents could be discovered for both teachers and students. How does this change in attitude start? For one thing, by applying the lessons in this book. Let's go back for a minute to the idea of judging wisely. That willingness to imagine others as people of great potential is powerful. And as we do that, we must also imagine ourselves in that same light. When we stop putting limits on ourselves and others, anything is possible.

My thoughts: Measuring intelligence is quite complex. My experience with this student and others left me questioning how many kinds of intelligence and abilities were left unmeasured and unrecognized. I even wondered what effect poverty and socioeconomic status had on an IQ test score. Over the years, I have come to believe that test scores are only part of a very big and complicated picture.

The bottom line is we all have our own unique gifts and talents.

One person might never write a book but can repair anything. Another can calm the wildest horse but may struggle with math. Some can sing while others can't even carry a tune. Someone can recall the birthday of every friend and acquaintance she has ever met but has such a bad sense of direction she gets lost inside the grocery store. Some of us are extroverts, with our own extraordinary gifts and talents. Others of us are introverts, with different strengths and interests.

Introverts seem to enjoy solitude. I do not enjoy being in large groups. I would find it difficult to be a good salesman. The differences among us abound. We are each unique.

I was teaching a couple of brothers how to handle a lariat by roping a bucket. The older brother learned what I was teaching him rather quickly. The younger one became flustered when he was unable to perform like his older brother. I told him that when I was in a roping competition, I often roped with those who were much better ropers than I was. But I never competed against the other ropers; I only competed against myself. I did the best I could do at the time, and that was it. Suddenly, I noticed a marked improvement in his roping.

We should not compare ourselves to others. By recognizing and placing a value on our own unique gifts and talents, we are able to build a healthier self-esteem. The only person you should compare yourself to is your past self. When we compare ourselves to the way we were yesterday, or last week, or last year, we can see our progress and the things we still need to work on, strengthening our belief in ourselves and our ability to magnify our own gifts and talents.

> *"Everybody is a genius. But if you judge a fish by its ability to climb a tree, it will live its whole life believing it is stupid."*
> —Albert Einstein

Comments from Nadine: Clients come to me because they are "stuck" in a place they don't want to be in life.

Often, I find it's because they are not working with their own personal talents or gifts.

While working at the Weber State University Counseling Center, one young woman was referred to me because she was not doing well in her prenursing classes. When I asked her why she wanted to be a nurse, she replied, "I promised my mother since I was a little girl that I would be a nurse. She always wanted to be a nurse but never had a chance."

As we talked about this in our next couple sessions, she kept bringing her latest sewing creations. She loved designing clothes and sewing them. She had won the "Make It with Wool" contest in high school. Still, she was determined to fulfill her promise to her mother to be a nurse.

That was until I had her spend a full day with a nurse friend of mine at the McKay Dee Hospital.

They were together all one Saturday. The following Monday when she came in for her appointment, I asked her how her day as a nurse had gone.

She looked disgusted when she said, "I threw up when I had to empty a bed pan. It was so gross." She further told me she had almost fainted when the nurse had her draw blood. They had to escort her out of the room when she turned white as a sheet and started to shake.

We processed all of this for a while. Then my client agreed it would probably be best if she changed her major to home economics with a teaching certificate. We talked about if her mother really wanted to become a nurse, she could try to arrange that for herself because that was *her* dream.

My client had a 4.0 GPA from then on until graduation. Last I heard, she was happily teaching sewing at one of the local high schools.

There are many kinds of intelligence. Most standard IQ tests, like the WISC, the Stanford-Binet, and others simply measure the ability to learn in an academic setting. They are the best we have for measuring that. They have proven statistically to be both reliable and valid. But they fall short of measuring intelligence in many other areas. I worked with a young man in the Weber School District who was doing poorly because he was sluffing school to stay home and work on completing the symphony he was writing. In our Options program, he could get high school credit for finishing his symphony. In return for that, he agreed to take the required core classes. This young man was not good in science or math, but he was a genius in music. My student at Weber State had a high IQ in sewing but not so high in nursing.

My belief is that everyone is born with a unique set of gifts and abilities. Each person's joyful task is to discover their personal abilities and then work to strengthen and magnify them so they can be used for everyone's good.

I love the idea of only competing with oneself. I was born into a musical family. My parents and siblings are all good at both singing and playing musical instruments. Unfortunately, I am tone deaf and can't always discriminate between notes. But that didn't stop me from trying to compete with them. I even worked hard and learned to play simple hymns and other pieces on the piano. I even worked at playing the cello and enjoyed that, though I probably was off-key a good share of the time.

And then one day I realized I loved public speaking. Whenever I am asked to speak about anything, I never write my talk. I simply choose the ideas I want to convey in my mind. Then, I know when I stand up I can speak in a way that holds everyone's attention. I speak as easily as I breathe.

Once I shared with a woman that public speaking was my hobby. She grimaced and said "Oh, dear, that sounds about as much fun as raising poisonous snakes." I'm sure she has talents and skills I can't even begin to touch, just as I have strengths and natural abilities that she doesn't. Once we learn to accept that we all have unique abilities and then honor and celebrate both our skills as well as the varied skills of other people, we will find that we progress in our own development and find true appreciation for the talents of others. When we reach that milestone, we will find true freedom, for we will have increased confidence and satisfaction in our abilities and greater appreciation for the abilities of others.

Your thoughts?

Your 21-Day Challenge

A 21-day challenge may be to begin building list of your unique gifts, talents, and achievements.

CHAPTER NINE

Opportunity

When given the opportunity to succeed, Duskee took advantage of the chance life handed him. What if, because of fear of the unknown, he had refused to go to Utah with Mr. Seeley? Look at the opportunities he would have missed.

Being on the football and/or basketball team opens doors for certain students, but membership on those teams is limited for obvious reasons. Before the high school rodeo club was established, the SideKicks could have experienced the tremendous satisfaction that comes from participation and competition in an athletic endeavor only in their dreams.

After their club was established, they found doors opened for them and wonderful experiences waiting to be had through one high school sport. And soon there was plenty of talk about the natural highs they were experiencing as they faced their fears at high school rodeos.

During a visit to North Sanpete, eight-time world champion bull rider Don Gay told the students about how he went about setting goals. When it came to overcoming obstacles, he would figure out how to overcome those obstacles one by one as they crossed his path toward achieving his goals.

He said, "If I needed money to pay my entry fee, I would do whatever it took to overcome that obstacle. I would even go to the stock contractor and tell him I would clean out his stock trailer or do whatever for him."

From my current vantage point, I can see that some high school students who seemed most likely to succeed still have not reached their expected mark. On the other hand, a few of the students who were not expected to succeed have excelled far above expectation.

This, no doubt, is due to many reasons. However, the one thing that stands out in my mind is fear. To overcome fear takes desire, grit, and determination. SideKicks were given opportunities to face fear head-on, which has had, no doubt, a positive carryover effect in their lives.

"When you want to grow, do something that scares you," urges Kristen Ulmer, former extreme skier and author of *The Art of Fear*. "You don't have to take suction cups up the side of a building. But taking risks is ultimately what proves to be the greatest for learning and growing,"[9] She is right. Risk means being willing to step outside of your comfort zone and try something new. It means sitting with the unpopular kid at lunch. It means learning a skill that doesn't come easily. It means practicing the new language you are learning, even though you know you will make mistakes. It means standing up for what is right, even if all your friends are afraid to stand with you. It means sacrificing some of your recreational activities and free time to work toward a dream.

Ramani Durvasula, professor of psychology at California State University, says leaving your comfort zone offers many benefits. It can "build efficacy, generate courage, and help people abandon self-doubt, and trust themselves a little more."[10]

My thoughts: The more one runs from fear, the more power fear has over that person. The SideKicks looked fear in the eye and took risks. As more opportunities opened up for them, they did not back down when the going got tough. They just kept moving forward. These traits have even continued to filter down into their families.

I shall never forget when fear overtook me as a teenager. A woman a year younger than I was had caught my attention. I had a buddy who had a driver's license and access to a car. I convinced him that we should drive past her house, which we did several times.

Finally, I built up enough courage to have him stop in front of her house. I guess I was hoping she might come out if she saw us. I was too fearful to go and knock on her door. As we waited, nothing happened. I'm pretty sure she and her family were watching us through their window. My buddy honked the horn, for I was too fearful.

Her father came out on the porch. I don't recall if one of us asked if she was home.

However, I remember him saying that the dogs were out back. We drove off. The next morning, I had to face him at school. He was one of my teachers. I never did get up the courage to ask her for a date. That opportunity was lost because of fear. Who knows what would have happened if I had overcome my fears? Perhaps she would have turned me down. But maybe she would have said yes. Don't let fear stop you from taking action toward the things you want in your life.

"Everything you want is on the other side of fear."[11]
—Jack Canfield

Comments from Nadine: If you run from fear, you give it power. You give it the power to steal from you the things that might have proven enjoyable or helpful if you had just exercised the courage to "feel the fear and do it anyway."

In the dark days after the attack on Pearl Harbor, Franklin Delano Roosevelt spoke to a nation of devastated citizens: "We have nothing to fear but fear itself." We overcame our fear, rallied to the cause, and consequently won the war.

Many opportunities are lost due to fear. We should acknowledge our fears because they are human and everyone experiences them at times. But we should also ask ourselves, "Is this activity something I would really like to pursue if it were not for my fear of doing so?" If the answer is yes, we need to find a way to overcome our fear.

As a professional counselor, I have helped many people overcome their fear of flying. Usually, they make an appointment with me to help them when they realize they are missing too many opportunities because of this fear. They miss seeing places or people they really want to see. Sometimes flying is the only sensible option for getting somewhere because other methods of travel take way too long.

I have helped people overcome other fears as well, including the fear of public speaking. One person I was never able to help with a major fear was my mother. Deep in her heart, she desired a college education. And she definitely had the ability to gain one. But she kept making excuses. When my father was alive, she thought he would not like her to do this. (Knowing him, he would not have minded at all. Probably would have been happy about it.) After he passed away, her excuse was "I'm too old to do that now."

When I was teaching at Weber State, I had several women in my classes her age or older. I told my mother I would help her register and that she could start with one class. I would even pay for it, and she could use my permit for the facility parking lot. But it was all to no avail. She said no to everything I suggested. Finally, she admitted she was very afraid of taking college classes and being on the campus. And she refused to stretch herself beyond those fears.

We should never empower our fears to keep us from opportunities to grow.

Your thoughts?

Your 21-Day Challenge

A 21-day challenge may be to seize an opportunity and not allow fear to intervene.

CHAPTER TEN

▲

The Power of Goals

Do you think Duskee set goals? Maybe not on paper, but I'm positive he had goals he worked toward. Otherwise, why would he have chosen to run in the deep snow in the middle of the winter prior to his track meets? He knew what he wanted: he wanted to win, and he kept a sharp focus on that goal.

With profits from the sale of calendars and other fund-raising activities, the SideKicks set a goal to purchase a bronc saddle for the club. With hard work and persistence, they eventually accumulated about $800 for their efforts.

We got in touch with a saddle maker recommended to us by world champion bronc rider Shawn Davis. When the saddle maker said he would bring the saddle to our school, our dream was in sight. It was not long before he showed up with it. And it had "NS SideKicks" engraved on its fenders. Called an "association saddle," it was designed to meet Rodeo Cowboys Association guidelines. With a full sixteen-inch seat, a rider could sit deep, lock his thighs under the swells, turn out his toes, and extend his legs to reach over the point of his bronc's shoulders with ease. We gathered around as he showed us how to adjust the stirrup leathers and get the right fit.

We finally had our own saddle—one with everything we had hoped for and more. We gladly handed him a check for $750. Our goal had been reached. A new door of opportunity had opened for the club members.

During Don Gay's visit to North Sanpete High School, he advised the Sidekicks "to discover what you want in life, set goals, and then put your best foot forward and make it stick. You can do anything you want if you believe in yourself and God." Don continued, "For my success, I surround myself with winners, think positive thoughts, set goals, and go for it. I give it 100 percent in all I do." He concluded by saying, "And, even above being a winner in rodeo is being a winner in life."

My thoughts: One of my early dreams was to become good with a lariat. During my teen years, I planned my roping arena. The only problem was, I never had the money to purchase the materials to build it. However, my dream and goal never vanished. Years later, when I did have the funds, my private arena was built, rope horses and practice cattle were purchased, and I became quite competitive as a team roper. That was when I learned the value of developing good habits. Some of the habits I worked on included following a sequence as I prepared myself to rope, visualizing myself making a perfect run before attempting the actual move, and learning to slow down and do things right. Most important, I had to learn not beat to myself up by trying to beat my competitors. I learned to compete only against my best self.

My father introduced the first quarter-horse stallion in our area back in the early 1940s. I grew up around good horses as he always had a band or two of good broodmares to run with his stallions. My goal was to carry on his tradition. After his passing, I ran around thirty mares and three stallions, and I marketed colts throughout the United States. Recently, I received a Twenty-Year Breeders Certificate from the American Quarter Horse Association. This was another dream of mine fulfilled by goal setting.

It's been said, "If you fail to plan, you'd better plan on failing." I've always enjoyed a good road trip. There's nothing quite like the freedom of the open road stretching out in front of you and getting to decide which direction you'll head, whether you want to stop at something interesting that catches your eye, or whether you want to explore a road that branches off unexpectedly. But even the most spontaneous road trip requires some planning. You've got to make sure you have some cash on hand, a few drinks and some food in the cooler, a spare tire, a map, gas in the tank, a great playlist, TP and sunscreen, maybe some charcoal briquettes and matches for a campfire, and a sleeping bag in case you end up spending a night under the stars. If a simple road trip requires planning, it's even more essential to plan your journey through life. I have discovered that we get out of life whatever we expect. In other words, if we don't set goals and expect to get the things we want out of life, we won't experience those things. Goals fuel our motivation to live a life of purpose and are the inner reason for living.

It sounds almost too good to be true: set goals and you'll increase your chances of reaching your dreams. And, of course, it isn't that simple. You need to apply effort. But goals done right can give you a tremendous boost. What do I mean by done right? I mean you need to set S.M.A.R.T goals. A smart goal is:

S—Specific
M—Measurable
A—Attainable
R—Relevant
T—Timebound

The most effective goals are specific, not vague. They state things in measurable terms. They must be attainable. This doesn't mean you can't dream big, but the bigger you dream, the more you need to break your goal into bite-sized chunks that can be reached in a reasonable amount of time. Making sure your goal is relevant is another key to successful goal setting. Be sure you are setting a goal that fits your values and know why you are committing to that goal. It's really tough to reach other people's goals. (For instance, if your parents want you to pursue a business degree but you are drawn to engineering.) That doesn't mean you can't consider input from people you value. Just make sure you are setting a goal for the right reasons and that it's true to your values and vision. Finally, a good goal has a deadline, one that challenges you to take prompt and persistent action, but there is also a realistic amount of time. (For instance, if your goal is to run a marathon, you don't want to set a target date of two weeks. Most experts recommend twenty.)

One more essential step in setting effective goals is to break each goal into smaller steps, and sometimes even smaller steps.

Let's take a look at how to put these steps into practice. Say you decide you want to get in better shape. If you set "Get in better shape this year" as a goal, you'll probably fall flat. It's too vague, for starters. Instead, apply SMART:

Specific: I will get in shape by walking twenty minutes a day, five days a week. On Saturdays, I will walk for forty-five minutes.

Measurable: this goal is now easy to measure because you can keep a log of the days you reached your walking goal.

Attainable: you've picked a reasonable goal—even if you're busy, it is possible to find twenty minutes a day for your walk, and you've scheduled your longer burst of activity for Saturdays, when you have more time.

Relevant: To really make this goal work for you, decide why you are doing it; for example, "I want to get in better shape because I want to hike to Delicate Arch with my friends." Having a clear vision of why you are doing something will help you reach it.

Timebound: My trip to Delicate Arch is in three months, so I will do this for the next twelve weeks.

This person is very likely to reach their goal, have a wonderful hike to Delicate Arch, and have increased confidence as they work toward other goals.

> *A final thought: "I don't focus on what I am up against. I focus on my goals and I try to ignore the rest."*
> *—Venus Williams*

Comments from Nadine: "How do you eat an elephant?" One bite at a time. Let me share an example of how breaking larger goals into smaller goals can help you reach your dreams.

I once counseled a young girl who had a goal of attending an Ivy League law school. But her grades were not good enough to be admitted to any law school, let alone an Ivy League school.

I noticed that she always got A's in classes she liked but poor grades in classes she didn't like. Often, she skipped attending these classes because they were boring. We talked about all the small goals she would need to achieve in order to reach her big goal.

We broke them down this way:

Start collecting A's in all classes by attending every day, taking notes, and studying for tests. (The goal was easy for her in her

English and history classes, but much harder in her math and science classes.)

Send away to her top five choices for law school and ask them to send her a list of requirements to be admitted to that school. Then choose a university where she could take all the necessary classes.

Continue her goal of earning as many A's as possible every semester in college.

Take the Kaplan course to help her pass the LSAT (the test you must take and get a high score on if you are to be admitted to law school). She should take this class early in her college career so she could begin taking the sample tests that would train her to get a high score on the test.

When her sample test scores were where she wanted them, she could take the real LSAT and send that final score to every law school she would apply to.

Figure out how much three years of law school would cost at each university. Then figure out how she would pay for that. She needed to be realistic and only apply for a law school she could afford.

Today this woman is a successful attorney, even though she went to a law school in Utah because that is what she could realistically afford. Sometimes goals need to be altered slightly to be realistic and doable.

Your thoughts?

Your 21-Day Challenge

An example of a 21-day challenge could be to set a big goal for yourself, then list the little goals that will help you to achieve your bigger goal. Plan how to overcome any obstacles that will interfere with you reaching your goal.

_____
_____
_____
_____
_____
_____
_____
_____
_____
_____
_____
_____
_____
_____
_____
_____
_____
_____
_____
_____
_____
_____

CHAPTER ELEVEN
Natural Highs

During the SideKicks' second high school rodeo season, they shifted into second gear. They aimed for greater winning opportunities while still fostering a spirit of excitement and enthusiasm. The SideKicks represented their high school at almost every rodeo throughout the state, becoming some of the most challenging competitors in the process.

It is difficult to measure exactly how much they had grown in self-esteem and self-confidence. But what was measurable was a noticeable improvement in their academic performance. Some were even graduating—something that wouldn't have happened without their participation in high school rodeo. As I noted improvement in their schoolwork, I began to wonder what their rodeo experience might do for them as they ventured into the arena of life.

Nearly forty years later, I asked Val, a former SideKick, why he chose to participate in all three rough-stock events. He said, "It was because of the rush it gave me. It was so fun, and I loved the challenge. I really wanted to get good at what I was doing. I was experiencing a whole new world with high school rodeo. High school rodeo became a drug. I had to be involved.

David, another SideKick, said, "That adrenalin rush was what carried me through my high school rodeo days. I went to the High School Rodeo Finals twice and then rodeoed two years after I graduated from high school. In fact, it was that adrenalin rush that carried me to driving demolition cars for fourteen years and then racing cars for another seven."

My thoughts: My son and I entered a Rope the Rockies Team Roping Series at the Sweetwater Fairgrounds in Rock Springs, Wyoming. We went into the final round in first place.

Then I missed a leg, and we ended up taking second. Coming home a little disappointed for missing first, we still experienced a natural high. We found we were looking forward to our next roping completion, eager to experience more of those natural highs.

Sometime after our Rock Springs experience, we were moving some horses from one pasture to another, and we had our trailer backed up to a corral in the neighboring community of Spring City. A middle-aged man approached me and asked, "Are you Reed Thomas? When I said yes, he said, "I want to thank you for saving my life." I had no idea who he was, but as he went on to explain our connection, I experienced a good feeling within, a natural high in a different sort of way.

Forty some years ago, I'd taught a class called "I Can" to a group of high school students using Zig Ziglar's book *See You at the Top* as the text. I barely remember this young man being in my class. At one point in our conversation, he chose not to continue his story. However, our brief encounter became one of those special moments in my life. When someone goes out of his way to thank you for saving his life, that is truly a natural high.

There are many ways to experience a high that is detrimental to our emotional and physical health. Drugs and alcohol are common ways people try to experience a high. The same is true for other negative and addictive substances and experiences, from pornography to risky behavior, such as shoplifting or street-racing, to name a few. Any high that comes from a negative behavior or addiction will always, sooner or later, lead to negative outcomes. That may be physical or mental or emotional damage, harm to yourself or other people, financial or legal problems, illness, and, in extreme cases, death.

Once you've experienced positive natural highs, you'll understand that they are better by far than the artificial highs you get from negative actions. Some of the best sources for experiencing a natural high include:

* Physical activity or exercise
* Creative endeavors
* Hard work in pursuit of a goal or dream
* Serving and helping other people
* Prayer or spiritual activity such as meditation and mindfulness

One thing you may notice is that attaining positive natural highs often requires commitment and effort on your part. In fact, this seems to be a rule of life: any good thing requires a price, generally in the form of hard work, persistence, patience, and commitment. But the great news is that it is always worth it in the long run.

Comments from Nadine: I believe we all get a natural high when we set a goal and then reach it. Often the more difficult the goal or subgoal, the stronger the high.

This type of natural high really increases self-confidence. I have found over and over again that if my clients succeed in meeting one goal, it gives them confidence to reach for the next.

I once had an experience with a recently widowed client. I did some grief counseling for a few sessions. Then I asked her if there was anything she had always wanted to do, something she hadn't done in her life yet. She thought about it and said, "You know, my ancestors came from Germany on both sides. I'm interested in genealogy, and I could do better if I spoke German."

I encouraged her to come to Weber State and take a German class. At first she was reluctant, but I told her she could always drop out if she didn't like the class. At first she found it difficult, but she kept studying, and at the end of the semester, she got an A. That gave her the self-confidence to keep going. She found she was gradually able to use it to do her genealogy.

She ended up taking all the classes we offered and then was unexpectedly asked by her bishop if she would like to serve a mission in Germany. When she returned from her mission, she finished college with a German-language major. She continued to work with the German community for several years.

There is no drug available that can compare to a natural high of reaching a goal by challenging yourself. When you use your agency to push out of your comfort zone and then are successful, that high boosts your self-confidence, which then enables you to keep stretching and growing. The best thing is, it doesn't require any special skills or resources. All it takes is making a commitment and working hard and refusing to give up. And once you see the benefits and experience those natural highs, you'll be hooked on a good thing.

Your thoughts?

Your 21-Day Challenge

A 21-day challenge may be for you to help someone or do something in which you experience a natural high.

_____
_____
_____
_____
_____
_____
_____
_____
_____
_____
_____
_____
_____
_____
_____
_____
_____
_____
_____
_____
_____
_____
_____
_____

CHAPTER TWELVE

Activities

Duskee made the best of his high school experiences. In spite of the hard work required on the family ranch, he still found time for music and track.

Athletic, academic, music, art, science, and community-service clubs are all an important part of the high school experience. They have important benefits, including bringing the community together and providing natural highs for youth, students, faculty, and parents. My biggest concern, however, is the students who do not get involved in athletics or any other extracurricular activities. I firmly believe that when students are involved in a positive activity, it helps them establish an identity, builds self-esteem, and gives them a sense of belonging. Beyond that, they experience some fun.

I met with some of the original SideKicks after several years had gone by. "We had so much fun," Jerry commented. "High school rodeo never gave me a bad experience. Even when I got hurt, it was not a bad experience. The thing that stands out in my mind coming from that experience is the camaraderie, the friendships we had with each other. We worked together and we helped each other. Often, it was nothing more than a box of saltine crackers and two dollars in our pocket."

Rusty agreed: "High school rodeo is the only thing that kept me in school. If not for rodeo, I would have lost interest. The camaraderie we had and the friendships we made, not only within the club but throughout the state, continue today.

"That rodeo program was good for all of us," Kelly said. "It has made us all better people. Those memories have become the highlight of our lives."

"Twenty years ago, Iceland had a problem. Its teenagers were among Europe's greatest abusers of drugs and alcohol. Now the majority of teens turn away from substance abuse and get a 'natural high' by spending more time with parents . . . quality time . . . and engaging in a greater selection of activities in sports, music, dance and the arts."[12]

Don't let excuses or worries get in the way your of being actively engaged in an activity during your high school experience. While it's true that certain activities require some funds or resources you may not have access to, it's also true that there are many activities that require little or no funding or special resources. It's also true that where there's a will, there's a way. If you are passionate about pursuing a certain activity, get creative and be persistent in finding ways to be engaged.

A great example of someone who persisted in following his dream is shown in the film *Rudy*—the true story of a young man who overcomes academic challenges (dyslexia), financial challenges (he's from a poor, working-class family with fourteen children), and physical challenges (he's only five feet six inches tall and a mere 165 pounds) to achieve his dream of playing for the Fighting Irish football team of Notre Dame.

While each of us has a different story and a different battle to fight, we can all relate to how tough it can feel to pursue a dream. But others' stories of success give us hope to hang on to until we reach our dream.

Another great film (and another true story) is *October Sky*, which tells the story of four high school students who created their own successful rocket and launched it in the 1950s, all by teaching themselves and pursuing an interest with persistence and passion.

If you are able to join an athletic or academic or club activity at your school, go for it. You'll gain so many great things from your experience there. But if you are in a situation where that is difficult for any reason, I encourage you to explore other activities you can start on your own or pursue with minimal funds or resources. One great example is competitive running. Marathons abound in every state, and many are geared toward beginners. Another option is short-course triathlons.

One young man recently signed up for the Spudman triathlon, and with no special gear, a borrowed bicycle, his old running shoes, and minimal training, he completed his first official race. As any competitor will tell you, it's a victory just to run or even just to finish. That young man came back the following year and improved his time by almost 50 percent. And if you are just getting started, the internet has many helpful articles and ideas to get you pointed in the right direction. In fact, if you are willing to put in the effort, you can start teaching yourself everything from coding and web design, to art and math, to engineering and construction. While all technology can be abused, and while internet technology has created the opportunity for negative applications, it's also a mind-boggling tool you can use in positive, powerful ways to expand your horizons, increase your opportunities, and create benefits for you and those around you.

My thoughts: Had I been more involved in sports during my teen age years, I feel I would have been less interested in taking the road I did. That road led me to becoming addicted to alcohol and tobacco.

I do regret that I did not get more involved in an extracurricular activity while I was in high school, however. Perhaps what I missed the most was the camaraderie. I was one of those outsiders looking in.

Later in my life, team roping gave me some of the experiences I had missed back in high school. Some of those real benefits included experiencing natural highs, developing my self-esteem and a sense of confidence, and feeling a camaraderie with others. Like many, I had my excuses at the time for not getting more involved: it was too expensive, too time-consuming, it didn't fit with who I had labeled myself as, I didn't have confidence in my skills, I didn't want to embarrass myself by showing what an amateur I was—You name it; I'm sure the excuse crossed my mind.

Whatever your excuse is, don't let it boss you around. You are in control of your decisions. You decide whether to act or not. Don't let fears, excuses, or false labels decide for you. One final thought for starting a new activity or project or pursuit. It can feel overwhelming at times, so here's a handy phrase to keep repeating: "Start where you are. Use what you have. Do what you can."

You don't have to be good to get started. That's why you are going to start—so you can get better. You don't need all the right equipment to get started. Use what you have, even if it's inadequate. And finally, do what you can, even if it's only one small step toward your goals or dreams. Doing anything is better than doing nothing.

Comments from Nadine: As a student, you'll spend about a fourth of your total time in school. Your other time is spent on eating, sleeping, exercising, personal grooming, and studying. But during the school week, that still leaves four to six hours for other things. At some point, you need to decide how you'll spend those "free" hours.

Some students use their free time to get jobs to finance their long-term goals. This can be invaluable. Working builds your résumé, teaches you interpersonal and work skills that may win over a future employer, helps you budget your time more effectively, and helps you save money toward education and other goals. These are valuable benefits should you decide to pursue this activity. But you can also reap many benefits from extracurricular activities.

In high school, I participated in debate and drama. In the process, I learned several skills that came in handy during my education and later my career. I learned a great deal about logic, how to organize and write an oration, and how to block out a play, memorize the lines, rehearse with the cast, and show up every night to be in the play for several performances.

For me, the natural high I got from winning kept me hooked on this exciting activity. I went on to win first place in the Daughters of the American Revolution oratory contest my junior year. Then I won first place in a Western States Dramatic Reading contest. I loved participating and reaching success in my goals. My debate partner and I took third place in the state's speech meet. We helped earn the points that gave Ogden High the first-place trophy that year.

My successful participation in the speech activities earned me a full-tuition scholarship to the University of Utah, and you may also find that your extracurricular activities will have similar, unexpected benefits. No matter what you do, as long as you are eagerly engaged in a worthwhile activity, you will gain positive benefits that continue on throughout your life.

Your thoughts?

Your 21-Day Challenge

One 21-day challenge may be for you to get involved in some activity within your school. Or you could choose to introduce an innovation that captures your interest as did the SideKicks.

_____
_____
_____
_____
_____
_____
_____
_____
_____
_____
_____
_____
_____
_____
_____
_____
_____
_____
_____
_____
_____
_____
_____
_____

CHAPTER THIRTEEN
Role Models and Mentors

Merriam Webster's definition: "A role model is someone who another person admires and tries to be like. A mentor is someone who is willing to spend his or her time and expertise to guide the development of another person."[13]

The Seeley family became Duskee's mentors. Duskee's role model was Mr. Seeley. As a family, they were there for Duskee. And Duskee was there for them. They looked out for each other.

Professional rodeo cowboy and national finalist Mickey Young had a positive impact on the SideKicks during his visit to North Sanpete High School. Not only did he teach them how to ride bronc horses, he also became a valued mentor.

Mickey tacked a note to the bulletin board that read: "Give 101% all the time." He also gave the SideKicks a large print of him riding a bronc. We decoupaged the print and placed it on our classroom's Wall of Fame. At the bottom of the print, he wrote: "Positive Attitudes are the Key to Success."

As a mentor, Mickey helped us understand what went into the making of a champion. He went the extra mile in showing the SideKicks he cared about them individually.

"While Mickey was in town, he dropped by our house," Jerry said. "He knew we were poor. My mother had paid for Val to take the seminar, but she couldn't pay for all of us. But Mickey never excluded any of us. We let him borrow our riding horses, and he gave us pointers. Mickey took time to help all of us."

Life is always a little easier with both role models to inspire us and mentors to show us the right path. Sometimes role models and mentors fall right into our life. Other times we have to go looking for them.

If you are lucky enough to have had role models and mentors handed to you, take advantage of the lessons and encouragement they offer. But you don't need to wait for a role model or mentor to show up. You can actively seek them out.

Role models can be found just about anywhere: church, school, work, and in sports and other activities. A role model will demonstrate the positive traits and actions you admire and want to apply in your life. Just seeing these positive traits in action can help you envision what is possible in your own life. Role models don't have to be rich or famous or obviously successful. Make it a goal to pay attention to everyone who crosses your path. Often, heroes are unassuming and quiet. That's illustrated by Medal of Honor recipients who, besides having demonstrated amazing courage in the line of duty, also demonstrate great humility and rarely talk about their accomplishments. If you could see into everyone's mind and heart and know their full life story, you would find that all around you are unsung heroes. Give people the benefit of the doubt, because heroes aren't always obvious, but they are there.

It's important to remember that even role models are human and make mistakes. No role model will be perfect in everything, and that's okay. Neither are you. Learn what you can from your role models, honor them for the good they represent, and forgive them for the things they aren't so great at.

An often overlooked source of role-model inspiration comes from good books. Great stories are often about characters who face difficult circumstances and overcome them by making righteous choices—brave-kind-compassionate-honest-difficult-but-good choices. If a character resonates with you because they demonstrate an admirable quality, they can be a good touchstone for the characteristics you want to develop in your own life.

While role models are often admired from afar, a mentor is more interactive. Again, you don't need to wait for life to send you the perfect mentor. Observe people who demonstrate a skill or quality you want to attain. Make sure this is a person you already have some valid relationship with (a teacher, coach, counselor, club adviser, community leader are all possibilities). Don't be afraid to ask for advice and guidance, but be respectful of their time. And don't be offended if your request is turned down. It may simply be that they are busy with too many other responsibilities. However, more often than not, people are happy to help.

Just as you can (and probably do) have more than one role model, you can also have more than one mentor, especially for the different areas of your life you are working on.

My thoughts: During his visit to North Sanpete High School, Don Gay said that for his success, he surrounded himself with winners. Mark Twain's words were, "Keep away from people who belittle your ambitions. Small people always do that, but the real great make you feel that you, too, can become great."[14]

After catching a steer in a team-roping competition or practice, it was always better to dally the rope around the saddle horn. This was more effective than just holding on to the rope with my hand. Since then, I have learned to also "dally up" to good models and mentors. I enjoy associating with those who empower me rather than those who bring me down. For those who tend to be toxic, I try keep some distance.

Comments from Nadine: I have been fortunate to have many role models and mentors in my life. As a young married woman, I would often find an older woman in our church or neighborhood that I admired. Then I would think about what it was about her I admired and work to implement those qualities in my own life. I don't believe any of those women ever knew they were my role models.

With role models, you can pick and choose those qualities you admire and leave the rest alone. But the whole idea has made me aware that someone may be watching me. So I have always tried to model positive qualities for anyone who may be watching. When it comes to mentors, I would never have been able to accomplish the things I have in my life without them. Four men in particular have mentored me far beyond any responsibility they may have had to do so.

Dr. Ronald Bingham, head of the Department of Educational Psychology at BYU, freely helped me through my master's and doctoral degrees. I would not have been able to finish my education and make the contributions I may have made to others without this outstanding man.

Jay Taggert, superintendent of the Weber County School District, gave me employment on two occasions after I made one phone call asking if he could use me and my talents in the district. His mentoring made it possible for me to do the research required for my doctoral dissertation.

Dr. Clyde Parker offered me a job as a psychologist for the Institute for Behavioral Medicine. During that time, Dr. Parker generously invited me to consult with him about any client I had while he freely gave me the benefit of his own education and expectations.

At a point in my career where I was experiencing burnout, I ran into Dr. Richard Southwick, director of counseling at Weber State University. He mentioned that there was an opening coming up and they would be hiring a new counselor. I applied and was accepted. During the next ten years I spent working with him, I had the best of all possible worlds.

I will always be grateful for those four men who went out of their way to mentor me. The only way I can repay them is to pay it forward by helping and being a positive mentor and role model to others. As you can see, there are many good people who are pleased to help you reach your goals. And, eventually, you can repay the favor by helping others along the same path.

Your thoughts?

Your 21-Day Challenge

A 21-day challenge may be for you to choose to be around those people who empower you in becoming a better you.

CHAPTER FOURTEEN

Giving and Receiving

Mr. Seeley gave Duskee a new hope in life. In fact, he gave Duskee the same hope and help he gave his seven other children. And Duskee continued to give back to the Seeley family. When Mr. Seeley almost lost his ranch during the Great Depression, a friend came to his rescue.

The SideKicks wanted to have a rodeo arena in their town but lacked the resources. Through their persistence, they were able to get a working grant. A working grant meant that the SideKicks and other community members would need to do the labor on the city's new arena and that the grant would pay for the materials. We were asked to draw up arena plans and submit them to Jim Thornton, the city council member in charge of the grant and our vice principal. The SideKicks began taking measurements.

They remain proud to have been a part of the rebuilding of the city's rodeo arena back in 1978. By way of their original petition for a high school rodeo, the new Mount Pleasant rodeo arena became a reality. It has since housed high school rodeos, 4-H activities, and the Hub City Days annual rodeo, in addition to many other horse-related activities.

Chief, a former SideKick, recently said that building the new arena back then was one of the things that gave him a new lease on life. As I ponder the services so many provide, I connect with Albert Einstein's quote: "Only a life lived for others is worth living."[15]

A couple I know in Alabama were on their way to Montgomery when they saw a man having car trouble along the side of the freeway. The woman said, "My husband and I pulled over to lend him a helping hand. Seeing his flat tire was beyond repair and he had no spare, we gave him a ride into Montgomery to purchase a new tire. We really went out of our way to help him get his car on the road again. We spent a good part of our day helping him with his problem. When his car was ready to go down the freeway again, he said, 'I am an airplane pilot. I can get you tickets to fly anywhere you want to go. Where would you like to go to?' With friends in Utah we wanted to visit, we said Salt Lake City. We had a wonderful vacation in Utah, all because we stopped and lent a helping hand."

My thoughts: Looking back through the years, the thing that gives me the greatest satisfaction is when I have forgotten myself and reached out to help another. Whenever I have reached out to others, rewards have come back to me in many forms.

My service to my community since 1975 has made a difference in some of the lives within this area. I did it without ever thinking of myself and how I might benefit. I just wanted to enrich the lives of others within the community as others had enriched mine. Near the end of June, 2017, I received a phone call that was the beginning of one of those rewarding moments in not only my life but in the lives of my wife and family. That call brought fun and joy into our lives as we also experienced gratitude and humility.

The lady on the phone said that as the event chairperson, she, along with the city council of Mount Pleasant, wanted to honor my wife and me as grand marshals in the annual Fourth of July Hub City Days parade.

A good friend provided his beautiful team of horses along with his new buggy to ride in. The city gave my wife a beautiful bouquet of red roses. A granddaughter said, "Let's get candy to throw to the kids along the parade route. Our other granddaughters quickly joined her. Five of my granddaughters joined us in the parade. Some rode on the buggy as they threw candy to the crowd while others walked behind throwing candy. As we rode that buggy down the parade route, we felt a lot of energy coming from the crowd along the way. The small role I played in enriching the lives of others and giving service to my community was well repaid in that ninety-minute buggy ride.

Who do you think benefits the most, the giver or the receiver?

Comments from Nadine: Giving and receiving are two sides of the same coin. You can't give without receiving something back, often more than you gave. I've personally experienced this as an educator.

I have known for a long time that if you learn something and then quickly share what you have learned with someone else, you cement that knowledge in your brain. So in sharing my knowledge with others, I benefit. You can apply this in your own life. If you study with a friend or a group and share your time and what you've learned, you'll find you understand the material better.

I remember when I was a little girl, my mother told me you never eat anything around anyone else without sharing what you are eating with them. Sometimes, a friend and I would each have a nickel. We would take the nickels to the grocery store for a popsicle. But if I wanted that ice cream treat and my friend did not have a nickel, I needed to take another nickel to treat her. (Yes, I did say nickel! Things have inflated much since I was a child over seventy years ago). What I learned was that being generous always led to stronger and better friendships.

There are plenty of other reasons to give. If you need a few selfish reasons to get into the habit of being generous, here are a few (backed by scientific studies):

* Giving makes you healthier.
* Giving leads to better mental health.
* Giving leads to greater success.
* Giving is linked with a longer life span.
* Giving makes you happier at your job.

Of course, the bottom line is that giving makes you feel great. Cultivate this habit and you'll have a more abundant life.

Your thoughts?

Your 21-Day Challenge

A 21-day challenge might be for you to do good without any thought of receiving something in return.

CHAPTER FIFTEEN

Innovations

By the beginning of North Sanpete High School Rodeo's forth year, several of the original SideKicks had graduated. It was bittersweet to realize they would no longer be representing our school as competitors. As they graduated, a few of them confided that they would have preferred to stay in school so they could high school rodeo another year. What a turnaround—some of students who didn't want to be in school at all now didn't want to leave. It took an innovative program to inspire this interest.

Innovation is best defined as a "new idea, device or method."[16] No matter who you are, innovation is a skill you want to nurture. All progress throughout human history started with innovation. Innovation depends on being able to think outside the box, to be willing to try new and unusual approaches and techniques, and to exercise your creative muscles. Innovation lies at the heart of all advancements in human history, including medicine, science, education, technology, and civil rights. But as grandiose as that sounds, you can use innovation in your own life to reach goals and achieve success at many different levels. Here are a few things to keep in mind about growing your innovation and creativity:

* We all have the capacity to be creative.
* Creativity isn't just for artists. Creativity can apply to any thought, activity, or goal—from sports to math to business to anything you can think of.
* Creativity can be learned.

Like all good things in life, it requires dedication, elbow grease, and, of course, practice. To get started, try reading a book (or three) for an introduction to some fun and amazing ways to develop this skill. Below are several ideas:

The Creative Habit by Twyla Tharp
Steal Like an Artist (10 Things No One Told You about being Creative) by Austin Kleon
Think Before It's Too Late by Edward De Bono
Zig Zag: The Surprising Path to Greater Creativity by Keith Sawyer

These are just a few of the many books that explore how to improve your skills in this area. If these don't strike a chord with you, get on Amazon and scout out a few other titles with the keywords *innovation* and *creativity*. You're bound to find one that fits your style and helps get you started on this exciting adventure. There are serious books, but there are also silly, fun, scientific, artistic, business, and scholarly books as well. It really doesn't matter. Any of them will be worth your time.

My thoughts: Years ago while living in Dothan, Alabama, I would often drive by a large statue of an insect, the boll weevil, in the neighboring community of Enterprise. I was told how, for several years, the boll weevil destroyed the cotton crops in that area, making it difficult for the cotton farmers to make a living.

They were forced to do something different to survive, so they began growing peanuts in place of cotton. The peanuts actually proved to be much more profitable. Discouraged cotton farmers with an innovation became motivated, even to the extent they raised a statue of an insect to honor their success. It just goes to show that creativity and innovation can come from the most unexpected places, even from defeat and disaster. In fact, some of the most creative innovations (like the light bulb) have come from repeated failure coupled with someone's determination not to let failure define them (or their ideas).

Comments from Nadine: We all enjoy the products of innovation and invention. For most of its history, the world did not have electricity and all that it provides. We did not have the telephone until Alexander Graham

Bell, and we did not have easily accessible home computers until innovators like Steve Wozniak, Steve Jobs, and Bill Gates used their creativity.

But while enjoying the benefits of these innovations, we sometimes fail to realize that without inventors we would not have things to make our lives easier and better.

And what kind of people were these innovators? They don't fit neatly into a mold. Several had some degree of autism that caused them to look at things in a unique way. Some, like George Washington Carver, were motivated by a desire to help right injustices. Others, like Alexander Fleming (inventor of penicillin) pursued their research because of personal experiences (Fleming had witnessed numerous deaths on the battlefield during World War I due to infections and hoped to find a solution.)

Most had to overcome skepticism and objections to their ideas. Grace Hopper was laughed at when she suggested computers could be programmed with everyday language. But her ideas led to the invention of COBOL, one of the first high-level computer programming languages. Innovation isn't limited by age, race, gender, culture, finances, education, physical health, or ability.

A quick internet search confirms there's a large number of teenagers who have created life-changing inventions or started successful businesses, many of them million-dollar ideas. One young entrepreneur (Mr. Cory's Cookies) got his start at age six. Thirteen-year-old Kylie Simonds is a cancer survivor who won a patent for her designer backpack, which gives chemo patients an alternative to clunky IV poles.

In recent years, teens have invented cheap ways to diagnose Ebola, purify water, dispense medicine remotely to elderly relatives who live far away, turn socks into tracking devices to keep Alzheimer's patients safe, and created a way to recharge your cell phone in twenty seconds. But hold on! Ninety-four-year-old John B. Goodenough is leading the research team working on a solid state battery that may revolutionize batteries for electric cars. And the oldest inventor to be granted a patent was 101.

Here's the essential thing you need to know: You can be an innovator too. You are capable of coming up with creative solutions for your life. You can learn more effective ways to improve your grades, your career skills, your relationships, your attitude, your success. And the first step starts in believing that you can.

Your thoughts?

Your 21-Day Challenge

A 21-day challenge may be to think of a new idea that will improve the way you live your life. That idea might be as simple as creating a habit of doing your hard homework first.

CHAPTER SIXTEEN

Things Are Hard before They Are Easy

It was undoubtedly hard for Duskee to adjust to a new family, a new lifestyle, new everything for the most part. But as time went on, things became much easier for him. This strange, new family and world became his home. It was the same with the SideKicks as they experienced rough-stock competition for the first time. It took awhile for things to come together for them.

David said, "When I rode my first bareback bronc, he threw me off pretty quickly. I didn't even come close to marking him out. In fact, it took me nine bronc rides before I was able to mark one out."

Brent, a local bronc rider said, "It took time and dedication to become really good at riding bucking horses. I had to make several bronc rides before I really got to where I could pick up my timing on a consistent basis."

It was when Wade drew Pepper that he experienced his first qualified ride after eight or ten disappointing attempts on other bronc horses. It was on that qualified ride he made a first-place win.

My thoughts: In a seminar in Minneapolis I attended years ago, positive-thinking pioneer Robert Conklin taught us how to take something hard and make it easier over time. He demonstrated how to deal with negative thoughts. He had the participants envision in our minds a beautiful, lush pasture next to a deep, bottomless pit. He then shared with us the fact that our mind can only deal with one thought at a time. As a thought enters our mind, we need to decide whether we want to keep it and put it out to pasture to grow or dump it overboard into the bottomless pit we create in our mind.

As I have applied this technique throughout the years, my thoughts have become more positive than negative. However, it took time for that habit to become solidified. It was hard before it was easy.

A second rule might be that things can be hard for a long time before they are easy. Ask just about anyone who has ever set out to learn an instrument. They will tell you it's true. It generally takes several years of practice to get even moderately competent at an instrument. It takes even longer to master it. But pretty much every single person who has learned to play an instrument will tell you it was worth it.

Here's another secret: as you work on hard things and they slowly get easier, they also tend to get more enjoyable. It gets easier to keep practicing and improving on the hard things, and so it becomes an upward spiral toward success. But in the beginning, it won't feel that way—your first run in preparation for a marathon, learning a foreign language, taking a coding class, making an effort to talk to people if you are shy, saying no to soda to reach a health goal, sacrificing to save money for college—no matter what challenge you face, it will be hard at first. But if you stick with it, it will get easier and you will achieve success.

That's why we should continue to strive to believe in ourselves, set goals, and follow our dreams. And to know that what we do will get easier as we move forward having a "never give up" attitude.

As I noticed with many of the SideKicks, it was not their gifts and talents that moved them forward. It was their grit and determination. That's a lesson for us all. Whatever we do that makes us stretch, whether it is writing a book, becoming more competitive in a sport or hobby, learning a new language, or achieving another challenge, it is our grit and determination that often brings our dreams to fruition.

Comments from Nadine: I love the wonderful feeling that comes from doing something well, but I don't like the necessary plodding and repetition that comes before that point. The truth is that practice and commitment are essential steps for improvement in any category.

I was not gifted at music, so I had to practice and plod daily for several years before I could play a simple hymn or Christmas carol. In my adult life, I have been grateful for that ability. It has come in handy when attending church services in countries and areas where few people had the opportunity to take piano lessons.

I also remember the hours of practice it took before I finally could ride a bike without tipping over. My poor mother would run beside me as I got the feel of it until one day she let go—and I rode it by myself! After that, I experienced the exhilaration of speeding along at a fast enough speed to feel the wind in my face and hair. It was so much better than walking or roller skating. The same was true with driving a car. For some it may come easily, but I spent hours in training before I could remember everything required. The day I finally got my driver's license was a day to celebrate. Driving was hard at first. But now I drive daily almost automatically, without giving the process a thought.

No matter what you start, don't give up when you realize it's hard. You'll gain great rewards by sticking with it.

Your thoughts?

Your 21-Day Challenge

Your 21-day challenge may be to have grit and determination in learning something difficult.

CHAPTER SEVENTEEN
▲

Stay the Course

No doubt Duskee never forgot the loneliness he experienced when his mother died. Or the hurt when his father traded him for a sack of flour. Rejection hurts. Duskee experienced obstacles early in life. However, as he stayed the course, he reaped many rewards.

The Duskee and SideKick stories seem to run parallel with each other. The morning after the State Finals Rodeo, the sun rose on new state champions. Among them were SideKicks Lauren and Blake. Lauren had taken second place in the second round on Honky Tonk Angel and ended up runner-up to Blake. They both had smiles on their faces. They now knew they were on their way to the National Finals Rodeo in Huron, North Dakota. At state, Blake was awarded a beautiful hand-carved saddle and a plaque that would make anyone proud. Lauren was given a buckle anyone would be proud to wear on a belt. He also received a couple of plaques.

Connecting with Blake after nearly three and a half decades, I asked him where life had taken him after high school. He said he'd continued competing in rodeo, then served a mission for his church. After that, he'd graduated from Brigham Young University with a major in finance.

As we reminisced about his rodeo days and as a member of the SideKicks, he talked about how important rodeo was in his life and what lengths he would have gone to so he could compete. "I considered it an honor to be at the National Finals. My parents were proud of me and my accomplishments. They supported me in everything I ever did in high school sports, but when it came to high school rodeo, they were reluctant. Now that they have both passed on, I guess it is fair to say that I would have forged their signatures if I had to so I could enter high school rodeos."

Blake placed second in the first go-round at the National High School Rodeo Finals in Huron. But in my mind and in his, he felt he should have done better. Today, his experience as a state champion was an experience never to be forgotten. Blake showed us that champions are made from something deep inside—a desire, a vision, and the tenacity in sticking to things.

My thoughts: In pursuing one's dreams and passions and in reaching a destination or a goal, the word *almost* does not quite cut it. Staying the course improves our odds of ending up at the mark we set for ourselves. Most successful people throughout history failed numerous times. One characteristic they had in common: they didn't quit. They tried again and again. To name a few:

> Abraham Lincoln failed numerous times in running for political office.
>
> Jack Canfield—Mr. Chicken Soup for the Soul himself—had his book rejected 144 times before it was published and went on to sell over 500 million copies.
>
> Oprah Winfrey was fired from her first television job but now owns a media empire and is ranked among the richest people in the world.
>
> J. K. Rowling was broke, divorced, and jobless before penning the book series that helped her become the first author to break the billion-dollar mark.
>
> Thomas Edison failed thousands of times in his attempts to invent the light bulb.
>
> Michael Jordan once said, "I've missed more than 9,000 shots in my career. I've lost almost 300 games. Twenty-six times I've been trusted to take the game winning shot and missed. I've failed over and over and over again in my life. And that is why I succeed."[17]

Almost every writer, athlete, scientist, inventor, artist, etc., has failed, often many times in many ways, before they achieved success. The great news is that you have access to the same key to success they did, simply by choosing not to give up.

Comments from Nadine: Staying the course means not giving up once you start something. Other words that describe this trait are *persistence*, *tenacity*, and even *stubbornness*. No matter what you call it,
  I believe that whatever it is that causes us to stay the course once we embark on it has a lot to do with passion—how strongly we feel about something.
  Whenever I feel passionate or highly motivated to do something, almost nothing can stop me. I make time for whatever it takes to do that thing. But without passion, I can rationalize that I just don't have time to do something, even though it may be a good thing to do. Intellectually I may want to do it, but without passion or strong emotion, I probably won't stay the course. One of my professors in college said, "Your students will learn something in direct proportion to the amount of emotion they have invested in it." I've found that to be true, both in teaching and in my own life. What I've observed is that if you have an emotional connection to your goal or dream, you're more likely to stick with it and succeed. Be sure you are reaching for a goal not because someone tells you that you should but because you are passionate about it. You can never succeed in trying to fulfill someone else's dreams for you.

Your thoughts?

Your 21-Day Challenge

Whatever your dreams or passions may be, they all have a beginning and, hopefully, the end you have in mind. Allow one of your dreams to have a solid beginning by staying the course for twenty-one days.

CHAPTER EIGHTEEN
Steer Your Mind

While attending bull-riding champion Gary Leffew's bull-riding school, the SideKicks had impressed on our minds the importance of taking control of our thoughts by having a positive attitude. As mentioned earlier in this book, Gary introduced us to *Psycho-Cybernetics* by Dr. Maxwell Maltz. *Psycho* refers to the mind, and *cybernetics* means steering—in other words, the book tells you how to steer your mind through positive thinking.

Gary had been told by his friend down in Texas that it would help his head. I thought if that book would help some guy's head, it might also give the SideKicks an edge in competition.

My thoughts: I have heard it asked, "How many thoughts can you think of at one time? Since our answer remains *one*, we only must control one thought at a time. If that thought is one we don't care to deal with, we can cast it out and make room for another thought. We can steer our mind the way we want it to go. That doesn't mean unwanted thoughts won't pop up. That's normal. Every person has experienced negative thoughts. A sibling may make us mad, or a setback may make us doubt our ability to reach a goal.

The important thing to remember is that you don't need to let unwanted thoughts stay. You can deliberately think about something else. You can deliberately choose where your thoughts reside. If someone says you can't succeed, you can dwell on those negative images, or you can push those thoughts away and imagine yourself achieving your goal. If a friend makes you mad, you can fan those flames or choose to focus on positive past experiences with that friend.

Since thoughts can be hard to lasso, a helpful tool is to say or write positive down sentences and phrases. These affirmations can help you to deliberately think positive and uplifting thoughts. So the next time an unwanted thought crosses your mind, put yourself in the driver's seat of your mind. Take a solid grip of the steering wheel and steer your mind to where you want it to go. And continue to enjoy the journey as you steer your way through your life.

> "Everything is created twice, first in the mind and then in reality."[18]

Comments from Nadine: Maxwell Maltz's book had a profound effect on my life. It has remained continually in print for the last six decades and has helped many to find success in all areas of their lives. While the language may be a little dated, the ideas in the book are practical and really work.

When I was first introduced to *Psycho-Cybernetics*, I was going through a difficult time in my own life. I had several young children and felt it was important to not work full-time while they were young, but I felt trapped. I began to experience some strange physical symptoms—heart palpitations, feeling like I couldn't catch my breath, and pain in my stomach. A trip to the physician assured me that there was nothing wrong with my heart, lungs, or stomach. But still, I sometimes felt like I was dying. Then I read *Psycho-Cybernetics* and realized I was causing most of my own symptoms with the negative thoughts I was thinking. I also realized I was in control of my thoughts.

I began to think more positive thoughts about my situation. When a negative thought crossed my mind, I focused on how healthy I was and how lucky I was to have four healthy, lively children. Although we were very poor at the time, my husband was in a postdoctoral program to become an orthodontist. I reminded myself that when he graduated, we would have enough money to buy a house with a yard where the children could play.

By changing my thinking, my physical symptoms disappeared completely. Many times, I have assured my clients and students that "thought proceeds emotion." If you're not happy with your feelings, change your thoughts. You'll be amazed at how your life improves.

Your thoughts?

Your 21-Day Challenge

A challenge might be to choose your thoughts more carefully. Take charge in steering those thoughts for twenty-one days.

CHAPTER NINETEEN

Visualize Success

In his bull-riding class, Gary Leffew told us how he had found himself in a slump when it came to riding. He said he was getting bucked off way too often. A friend recommended *Psycho-Cybernetics*. In this book, Dr. Maltz explains that the mind cannot tell the difference between a vividly imaginative experience and the real thing.

Gary decided to grab his fishing pole and head to the hills. There, he rode bulls in his mind. "I would visualize those bull rides in my mind, their sounds, and my own moves and counter moves as I saw in my mind me making a winning ride," he said. "When I came out of those woods, I was hot. I felt I could ride any bull."

Gary taught us that as we visualized success, we could become successful in our lives. He helped bull riders to see themselves making successful rides and to believe in themselves becoming successful not only in the rodeo arena but also in life.

This concept of visualizing success has had a lasting effect on me and the SideKicks. When I first arrived at North Sanpete High School as a teacher, few of those students who later became SideKicks ever considered visualizing success in their minds. Their focus was simply to make it through another day of school. After becoming active participants in rodeo, they began seeing life through a new lens of renewed self-confidence, self-esteem, and hope for themselves.

Soon after the building of the new indoor Contoy Arena in Mount Pleasant, we sponsored a bucking-bull competition, with breeders of bucking bulls transporting their bulls from as far away as Hawaii. I was amazed at how well these bulls bucked. Most of the riders were thrown off their bulls in less than five seconds.

When I said to Dean, one of the original SideKicks, "No one can ride some of those bulls for a full eight seconds," he looked at me and said, "Reed, there is no bull that can't be ridden."

Gary Leffew had made a connection with him on the value of visualizing success. And I learned another valuable lesson from a SideKick.

My thoughts: At a training I attended in Minneapolis, Minnesota, Robert Conklin introduced the 3 *V*s: visualize, verbalize, and vitalize (see, feel, and say your success.) Visualization, I learned, is *seeing* it done right before you do it. Then you *tell* yourself what you want to see, building your self-confidence. Then you *feel* from the inside what you want to see on the outside. That is the 3 *V*s in a nutshell: visualize, verbalize, and vitalize.

I found this concept to be most helpful with team roping. After each practice, when I was alone, I would relive my misses in my mind. Those misses would become winning catches. I would even tell myself how good that catch was as I practiced on the ground and visualized it being a real run. Then I would visualize myself making a successful run. That continued to help me become a better team roper, even putting me in the winner's circle once in a while. Team roping became a mental game to me.

While I attended Utah State University, my roommate had a full-page picture of a new 1966 Buick Toronado automobile attached to his door. Once he graduated in civil engineering, he was seen driving that new 1966 Toronado. A friend built a small wagon to be pulled by his team of pulling ponies. At night, he would vision how he was going to continue with his project the next day. Eventually, what he saw in his mind became the finished product.

Years ago, I met Muhammad Ali in Las Vegas, prior to his championship bout with George Foreman. He kept repeating over and over to us, "I am the greatest!" He became known for visualizing his success in winning a fight.

He continued to retain his title as the world's heavyweight champion. A couple years later, Muhammad Ali took on an underdog, Chuck Wepner. It was a fifteen-round fight. In the ninth round, Ali received a punch from Wepner that put him down. It looked as if the fight was over. Then Ali recovered, got up, and when on to retain his title. The vision he had of winning that fight garnered another win for him.

Comments from Nadine: If you can relax and clearly visualize something, it will actually impact the brain the same as if you were doing it. In this way, you can program your brain to be able to perform that task easier and better.

Our brains are like highly technical, beautiful, refined computers. We can program our computers to do whatever we want them to do. And I believe we can program our minds the same way.

I once worked with the girls' track team at Weber State University. I spent time talking to each girl about what she wanted to accomplish at the next track meet. I made sure their goals were realistic for them.

Then I had them lean back and become very relaxed. While in that state, I had them visualize the next track meet. They pictured what they would be wearing. They pictured being relaxed before the actual race.

Then they pictured going up to the starting line, getting their feet in the correct position, and listening carefully for the starting gun to fire. At that point, they visualized themselves running swiftly and smoothly. They would run very fast while still having a relaxed and positive mind.

They would not pay attention to the others on the track, only to their own smooth, fast speed. Finally, they pictured themselves crossing the finish line and hearing that they had reached their speed goal and beyond.

These girls came to my office three times a week in the month before the track meet. On the day of the track meet, they not only reached their goals, many even reached new personal bests. Weber State took the trophy that year in girls' track.

I have used this relaxation and visualization technique to help clients program their minds for success in a variety of ways. It works well in helping someone overcome a fear of flying in an airplane. Others have used it as part of an integrated strategy to lose weight. We can boost our own effectiveness in all our goals by using the power of the subconscious mind and by visualizing success.

Your thoughts?

Your 21-Day Challenge

A 21-day challenge might be to use the three Vs to improve your performance in an area of your choosing.

CHAPTER TWENTY

Resilience

Resilience is the ability to become strong, healthy, and successful after something bad happens; it's the ability to recover from or adjust easily to misfortune or change.

Duskee knew what it felt like to get bucked off a horse and then climb right back on. He had that "bounce back" attitude. He had been through the school of hard knocks at an early age. His story is an example of great resilience. Another example of resilience comes from one of the SideKicks.

Eighteen months had passed since Shorty, a bull rider, was involved in a car collision with a train. In that accident, he split his head and broke a bone near his left eye, close to his optic nerve. He also broke his arm and leg and punctured a lung.

As the annual Pioneer Days Rodeo approached, he decided to enter. This would be his first bull ride since his nearly fatal accident. It would take place in his hometown, where he had a lot of fans to cheer during his ride.

Shorty said, "When the announcer mentioned the next bull rider was me on bull #76, I heard screaming and hollering throughout my ride. There was so much noise I couldn't even hear the whistle blow."

Also recalling the ride, fellow SideKick Jerry said, "I was there and saw it all happen. That rodeo crowd became totally ecstatic. Even Bill, who seemed to enjoy watching riders being thrown from his bucking stock, was rooting for Shorty. It was obvious Bill was hoping with the rest of us Shorty would ride that bull for the full eight seconds."

"I felt for Shorty," Bill said. "I had visited with him when he was in the hospital. This bull was no joy ride—#76 had a set of horns that came out of his head upward. I called them devil horns. Shorty made a beautiful ride on that bull. He even stuck some iron into that bull during his ride."

After Shorty had covered his bull for a full eight seconds, he heard a deafening roar from the spectators. He ended up splitting first place with another bull rider. "That was an experience I will never forget," he said.

Shorty's ability to come back and fight through his fears was evidence of mental toughness. This definition of toughness doesn't involve physical strength or size but being able to withstand something without showing weakness. Shorty showed toughness through his comeback. He faced a challenge head-on as he remained honest to himself and his wellness. To do what he did took incredible strength and resilience.

We all have the capacity to be resilient; it's a skill that can be developed and strengthened. Here are three habits resilient people use to help them in tough times:

1) Resilient people understand that tough times will always come to an end, sooner or later. It may not seem like it when you're wading through the manure, but it's totally true. The sun always rises. Spring always follows winter. Resilient people keep taking one step after another and eventually find that they've turned the corner and things are looking up.

2) Resilient people practice gratitude on a daily basis. No matter how bad you think you've got it, someone somewhere has it worse. Always. The old quote "I cried because I had no shoes until I met a man with no feet" may be cliché, but it's true. Numerous studies show that people who practice gratitude win in a number of ways. They are happier, have more friends, less stress, better relationships, get sick less often, live longer, are more productive at work, and are, yes, more resilient.

3) Resilient people focus on the positive and take action on the things they can. They may not be able to fix every part of what's going wrong in their lives, but they choose to believe that things will get better.

My thoughts: Through their high school rodeo experience, the SideKicks learned how to be resilient, to endure pain, and to use it as fuel to press forward. Even when they were not winning, they stayed focused on pursuing the dream of winning.

As adults, the SideKicks were prepared to move forward when hit with obstacles ranging from divorce to unemployment to illness. They had acquired the tools to convert life's setbacks into present-day success stories. Even those SideKicks who had to deal with learning disabilities learned how to compensate, remain positive, and think well of themselves. They had acquired a mind-set of making the most of life despite of the obstacles thrown in their paths.

You can do the same thing. I challenge you to look at the tough times life throws at you as an opportunity for success, not a guarantee of failure. You are in good company. Every single person who has found success first failed at something. But they kept going until they reached their goal. You can too!

Comments from Nadine: Resilience is an important skill to master. Sooner or later, everyone is going to experience some unwanted misfortune. If we are resilient, we can figure out a way to bounce back and go on with our life and goals.

One example of this is receiving a poor grade in a subject. Allow yourself to not like it, but vow to do better next time and decide how you will do better. This way you become more resilient and better prepared to turn future challenges into successes.

When my granddaughter graduated from high school, she was accepted to an Ivy League school on the East Coast, Brown University. We were all excited for her, and she left with a great deal of enthusiasm.

School wasn't difficult for her, but living away from home was. She had always lived in Salt Lake City in a close-knit, loving family in a comfortable home with her own room and bathroom. She had the support of extended family members and friends.

Suddenly she was clear across the country where the houses were different. She was living with a roommate she couldn't relate to and eating foods that were different than she had at home. Predictably, she was quite homesick. She felt like a fish out of water. And it wasn't comfortable.

But she allowed herself to acknowledge the stress, accept it, and resolved to stay the course, at least until the Christmas break. When she made it that far, she decided she could handle one more semester. This time it was easier, and she made friends on campus.

She persevered and was able to graduate from Brown University and is now preparing to enter veterinary medicine school. Anna has become resilient enough to be able to live wherever she chooses.

Anyone can learn resilience by doing difficult things until they become easy.

> "Our greatest glory is not in never falling, but in rising every time we fall."
> —Confucius

> "Promise me you'll always remember: You're braver than you believe, and stronger than you seem, and smarter than you think."
> —Christopher Robin to Winnie the Pooh[19]

Your thoughts?

Your 21 Day Challenge:

A 21-day challenge may be to make a conscious choice to bounce back when you get knocked down by life or depressed or discouraged. Face your challenge head-on. "Cowboy-up" and continue your ride.

_____
_____
_____
_____
_____
_____
_____
_____
_____
_____
_____
_____
_____
_____
_____
_____
_____
_____
_____
_____
_____
_____
_____
_____

CHAPTER TWENTY-ONE

Affirmations

The Sidekicks' story began when certain high school students became participants in the SideKick Club. It ended four decades later when they were adults with their own families and even grandchildren. I had the privilege of watching and living among many of them throughout those years.

As their high school rodeo adviser, I was able to watch good boys go on to become great men. It occurred to me that some of those SideKicks could become the first in their families to attend college. That struck me with force, as I was a first-generation college student myself.

I also saw good boys with great potential, which, on the surface, was something difficult for some to see.

When high school rodeo was introduced, those who became active competitors began seeing themselves as winners. This affirmation carried them past their high school days.

It's been a privilege to watch them become not only winners in the rodeo arena but also inthe arena of life.

Being involved in high school rodeo was life-changing for the members of SideKicks. Many went on to honorably serve their country in the armed forces. Now they and others continue to serve our great nation in their area of expertise, their families following their example of being good citizens. I have witnessed affirmations become reality as the SideKicks saw a better future for themselves.

My thoughts: Kelly said, "High school sports never really interested me, but I did like to keep in shape, so I stayed fit for high school rodeo. In fact, I became pretty good at skipping rope in PE. I could cross over and even skip on one foot." After four decades, I met Kelly and his grown son at a restaurant. During our visit, I asked Kelly if he would do a skip-the-rope demonstration for us. I wish you could have seen the look on his face as he said, "Come on, Reed!" Then we enjoyed a good laugh together. Time does change our physical abilities. However, we all can remain affirmative as we continue to envision our best selves moving forward for a better future.Growing up, I enjoyed Norman Rockwell's paintings on the covers of the *Saturday Evening Post*. Even in troubled times such as those Depression years, his paintings showed the goodness of life. He once said, "I paint life as I would like it to be."[20] That's a message for us to continue to be affirmative in seeing things the way we want them to be.

Beginning with the end in mind[21] causes one to think ahead with his/her life. Where will you be in five, twenty, or even forty years? What will life be like for you then? Affirmations are positive statements that help you reach your goals and become your best possible self. That's because we are all capable of great things, but the world often fills us full of negative messages and doubts. Focusing on the positive by repeating supportive affirmations can be a shield against negative criticism. Affirming is as easy as writing down the positive outcome you want or describing yourself in a positive way. For instance: "I am strong and confident." "I control my choices and actions, so I can succeed at anything I set my mind to."

Comments from Nadine: An affirmation can be something you repeat about yourself that you want to be true. It may be only partially true at the time you start saying it, but if you keep repeating it, it often becomes true.

It's a good way to program your mind. If you visualize the affirmation along with repeating it, its ability to create positive outcomes in your life and behavior increases.

I use affirmations for myself, and I teach my clients to repeat them for themselves. Whenever I'm going into a potentially stressful situation, I mentally repeat, "I am relaxed and peaceful." As I repeat it, I can feel my shoulders relax, and my muscles become loose, and I feel freer. My breathing becomes deeper and slower. Any tension is simply gone.

This works well for any feeling you would like to experience in any situation. It is especially good for controlling anger in a situation where you have become angry in the past.

You may simply say, "When I see that person, I will be smiling and politely kind no matter how that person treats me."

You can't always control the future by affirmations, but I have been surprised at how often I have seen it happen. A young woman came into my office on a Friday afternoon before I was going to be gone for a week on vacation. She was very upset, telling me, "I am a senior in college, and I came here hoping to find the right man and get married during my college years. I am going to graduate in a few months, and I'm not dating anyone." The situation was making her depressed and anxious because she was about to go back to her own small town and work in her parents' business. She was not likely to meet anyone new there. I had another client right after this woman, so I couldn't give her extra time, but I felt like affirmations might help her until I could see her ten days later. I gave her a penny to put in her shoe. I told her whenever she felt that penny as she walked, she was to repeat, "I am attractive and smart. Soon I will meet the person I am going to marry." That was it, except she was to attend all the Friday-night dances held for singles at the church she attended. Then I rescheduled with her for the week after I returned.

I left for vacation the next day, and when I got back, the young woman did not show for her appointment. I was very busy after being on vacation, and I soon forgot about her. About six months later, I ran into her at the grocery store. She came up to me and said, "Do you remember me?" She looked vaguely familiar, so I said what I always do, "You look familiar, and I know I should know you, but tell me who you are." She then updated me about how she was the one who'd worn the penny in her shoe. I remembered her because I had never suggested that technique before.

At that point, she showed me her engagement ring. She said at the very next Friday-night dance she attended, she met this really nice guy. They started dating, and now they were engaged to be married in a few months.

I will never know if it was the affirmation or the penny or just luck, but I always felt it was more than coincidence. In fact, I was so convinced the affirmation helped that even to this day I keep a small dish of pennies in my office. I don't give affirmations to everyone I see, but where appropriate, I hand clients a penny for their shoe and we come up with an appropriate affirmation. And I still use affirmations for myself. (I even walk on a penny now and then.)

Your thoughts?

Your 21-Day Challenge

An example of a 21-day challenge might be for you to begin seeing yourself as you want to become.

CHAPTER TWENTY-TWO

A 21-Year Challenge
by Rod Miller
(Rod is an award-winning writer, author, and poet. I asked if he would share his journey of success in life.)

Reed Thomas speaks my language. Having grown up with cattle and horses, and competing in high school, college, and professional rodeos as a young man, Reed's stories in *SideKicks: Helping Youth Succeed against the Odds* ring true to me. *SideKicks Challenger: 21 Life-Changing Challenges to Empower Teens* puts the lessons learned into motivational challenges that apply to every life, whether you are a teenager or an adult like me, who measures his age in multiples of teen years.

Nowadays, I spend most of my writing time writing about the American West or dealing with the ins and outs of seeing what I write put in print. To date, publishers have applied ink to my words in the form of six novels, four history books, three collections of poetry, a collection of short fiction, and scores of articles in magazines.

The thing is, I have no training or education in creative writing. I never took a class in writing fiction or poetry or any kind of writing other than journalism, in which I earned a degree.

But, even at that, I never worked in journalism. I spent my working life writing advertisements.

You know—all those annoying ads that clutter up magazines and newspapers, those commercials that interrupt what you trying to watch or listen to on your TV or radio, and those ugly billboards along the highways.

It was a good career. I enjoyed it and had a good deal of success at it. But even with all the millions of words I put on paper in advertising, I never considered myself a "real" writer. I was just an advertising copywriter. "Real" writers wrote the books I loved reading and read endlessly.

One day as I approached middle age, for reasons I still don't understand, curiosity grabbed hold of me, and I wondered if I could write a poem. A poem, naturally, about cowboys. Even after living in the city for years, the cowboy life was still near and dear to me, so writing about cowboys and the West only seemed natural.

That curiosity turned into a self-induced challenge to write poetry. I studied poems. I liked to figure out what made them work and put those lessons to work in writing my own poetry. Soon enough, my poems started appearing with some regularity in magazines like *American Cowboy* and *Western Horseman*.

The next curiosity-driven challenge I set for myself was to write short stories. I still had no illusions that I could write a book. But a short story? I'd give it a try. Several of my stories were accepted for publication by some big-time editors and publishers.

Getting my poems and stories published encouraged me, and eventually my curiosity had me accepting the challenge to write a book. A whole book. Intimidating, for sure. But maybe, just maybe . . . Then I did it. And I did it again and again.

Meanwhile, writing for magazines over the years has allowed me to do a lot of interesting research and interview a lot of interesting people and learn a lot of interesting things. My curiosity continues to challenge me to learn about new subjects and people and places and events I want to write about, whether in books or stories or poems or magazine articles.

And to write.

The challenge to write has lasted twenty-one years so far. It shows no sign of letting up.

What's the biggest lesson I've learned? Don't be afraid of your own curiosity. It's the only cure I know for ignorance. It will challenge you to learn and do things you never imagined possible. And, as Reed Thomas will tell you, challenges are good for you.

My thoughts: As we accept challenges, we need to have the tenacity and willpower to stay committed. Rod has shown us how he has continued pursuing his passion for twenty-one years. From my viewpoint, he has mastered the ability to write well as a result.

It didn't come without a price or without effort. But by accepting challenges, never giving up on his passions and goals, he is now enjoying what he envisioned twenty-one years ago.

Today becomes a new beginning for a better tomorrow for both you and me.

Comments from Nadine: Curiosity, passion, and tenacity are all vital in using our talents to grow and to serve others in the process. Rod Miller used these tools to rise step by step. When we climb a ladder, we don't leap from the bottom to the top. We start at the first rung and climb at our own speed until we get there. Then, when we are at the top, we are comfortable with being there.

We go up step by step in climbing both ladders and mountains and in growing in life. For many years one of my hobbies has been hiking. I've climbed to the top of many tall mountains in Utah, but I will never forget my first tall mountain.

At the age of fourteen, I climbed to the top of Ben Lomond peak. It was a long and very difficult hike at my age, and the cheap shoes I was wearing made it even harder. I became very tired and was tempted to stop several times. We had one young leader, and he had to leave us halfway to carry a young girl back to camp when she became injured. He told us to wait exactly where we were for him to return.

I was on a ledge about four feet wide while I waited. I was tempted to go back to camp with our leader. Instead, I used the waiting time to pray for physical and mental strength to make it to the top.

When our leader returned, I put forth great effort and made it to the top, where I could put my name in a metal box containing the names of those who had made it. Later, back at camp with sore blisters all over my feet, I was so happy to have done something difficult that I vowed I would climb other mountains in the future.

Your thoughts?

CHAPTER TWENTY-THREE

Your Life Story

Each one of us is capable of living an amazing life filled with adventure, service, and purpose. We'll all have obstacles to overcome if we are going to create the life we are meant to live. It can be tempting to look at others and think they have it so much easier—maybe they have more money or better health or more opportunities. Maybe they have a supportive family or social connections or better education. There's no doubt that some people have advantages others don't. But here are a few truths to keep in mind: 1) No matter how privileged someone else may seem, every single person has their own, often-unseen struggles. 2) If you play the comparison game, you will never rise to your own potential. 3) You have incredible power in the form of your choices. You can change your life by making better choices. You can pick yourself up and try again if you make a poor choice or a mistake. You can always take a different path if the one you are on is not taking you to the life you wanted. You may not have the perfect environment or family or money or health or the exact set of skills and talents you would like, but every single person who has ever accomplished anything worthwhile in life also had disadvantages, no matter how easy they appeared to have had it on the surface. When you understand that you have great power in the attitude and actions you choose, you can accomplish great things.

Dr. Stephen Covey wrote *The 7 Habits of Highly Effective People*, a powerful book that includes a timeless set of tools to help anyone succeed in life. One of the habits is "Begin with the end in mind."[22] You can't reach a destination if you have no idea where you are going. The same is true with your life and goals. You can't succeed if you don't have a clear idea of what you want to accomplish and what that will look like.

One way to get that clear picture is to imagine your life ten, twenty, thirty, or more years down the road. I suggest writing it down. This makes it more real and impactful. Write down where you would like to see yourself. Where do you live? What work do you do? How does it provide for you and your family? What contributions have you made for others? What talents have you developed? In what ways have you served others? How have you grown mentally, spiritually, emotionally, financially, and physically? How have you shared your success with others? How many have you helped along their own path? What relationships have you developed and nurtured?

Move back through your years, envisioning the good choices you made that put you where you see yourself now. Bring to life your dreams, passions, and goals. Write down how you see your future and your future self.

Once you have that picture firmly in place and with your dreams, passions, and aspirations in mind, write down your life goals, beginning with where you are now.

Plan how to overcome any obstacles you foresee. First write your big goal, then list any supporting goals that will help you achieve your big goal. (The goal ideas in chapter 10 can be helpful as you complete this exercise.)

With this vision and these goals as a roadmap, you can start your life adventure with confidence. You're off to great things.

My thoughts: As a schoolteacher, my heart continues to bleed as I see past students making poor choices. Through the years, I have seen those poor choices lead to their downfall and even to an early death. I rejoice when I see others succeed, even against great odds, by making good choices. For these reasons, I've chosen to write the story of the SideKicks and its sequel.

Hopefully, my efforts will help someone, somewhere, to have a richer and more satisfying life.

By making better choices, by following one's inner guidance system—that gut feeling—and by applying some of the challenges contained within, lives will be enriched.

Looking back, the what-if moments are what come into focus as I grow older. Those what-ifs allow me to see the many different roads my life could have taken. Some of those what-ifs are chilling.

Toward the end of George Bernard Shaw's life, a reporter challenged him to play the what-if game.

"You have been around some of the most famous people in the world. You are on a first-name basis with royalty, world-renowned authors, artists, teachers and dignitaries from every part of this continent. If you had your life to live over and could be anybody you've ever known," the reporter asks, "who would you want to be?" Shaw responded, "I would choose to be the man George Bernard Shaw could have been but never was."[23]

I too could have done more. I could have become the man Reed Thomas could have been but never was. Think about your life as it moves into those twilight years. What might your response to that question be? What would you like that answer be? Just give it some thought.

We all have different missions and purposes in life. The what-ifs are what can make or break us.

"I say be the hero in your own movie. Pretend that your life was a movie and it started now. What would the hero do? What would the person you represented do? What would the person you admire and inspire do?"
—Joe Rogan[24]

Comments from Nadine: Imagining your future can be an incredibly helpful exercise in helping you create the life you want to live. Evaluate where you currently are and then think clearly about where and who you want to be in ten, twenty, thirty, or even forty years.

After that, identify the changes you need to make to be on the path you've envisioned for yourself and set a timeframe for making those changes.

I think it helps to clearly visualize yourself making whatever changes need to be made. Then write what you want your personal life story to be twenty or forty years from now. One way to do this is to pretend you are writing your obituary. It may sound a little macabre, but it makes it real to put on paper what we want to accomplish before we die. Cast your thoughts into the far future. Imagine you are ninety or even one hundred. What have you accomplished? Who did you help? What did you contribute to the world? How many lives did you improve? How did your dreams play out? Imagine your friends and family and how you've contributed to them reaching their goals and dreams as well, because in the end, that is what will matter most. What legacy will you leave?

Your thoughts?

CHAPTER TWENTY-FOUR

Golden Reconnections: The SideKicks Legacy Lives On

"There are some things which cannot be learned quickly, and time, which is all we have, must be paid heavily for their acquiring."
—Ernest Hemingway[25]

Thursday, July 20, 2017, a headliner in the local newspaper, *The Pyramid*, read:

Rusty Bench named grand marshal of Fairview Horse Parade. Rusty was a founding member of SideKicks, the North Sanpete High School Rodeo Club from 1976-78. This is where he began bull and bronc riding, which started his rodeo career of 14 years. He won many events including the All-Around Cowboy award in the spring of 1978 at the SideKicks High School Rodeo and to this day he still proudly wears his SideKick belt buckle. The SideKicks were instrumental in putting up the rodeo arena in Mount Pleasant in 1977.

Bench has served as a Fairview City Councilman for 10 years, overseeing the Fairview City Pioneer Days celebration for eight years and in charge of the rodeo itself for 10 years. He also spent significant time on the committee to oversee the Demolition Derby and oversaw that event for 14 of the first 18 years. Rusty also served as president of the local snowmobile Association for four years and a member for 12 years. Mostrecently, Bench has served on the Sanpete Travel Council. Bench also served as director of the Contoy Arena in Mount Pleasant for three years."[26]

Rusty said, "High school rodeo is the only thing that kept me in school. If not for rodeo, I would have lost interest in school. We had so much fun. That experience has created some good memories for me, which linger on."

The members of SideKicks agree that the lessons they learned in the club had a positive impact in their lives after high school and beyond.

Val felt like the SideKicks Club changed him for good. He said, "During my junior and senior years, high school rodeo gave me a reason to stay in school. Those couple of years made a difference in the direction my life has gone. It gave me a reason to face life's challenges without fear. I quit being afraid as high school rodeo turned loose the adventurous side of me. It allowed me to grow and become the person I am today.

"You helped me as we interacted together," Val said to me as I visited with a few of the SideKicks one day. "You and that high school rodeo experience shaped the life I enjoy today—a good wife, a married thirty-four-year-old daughter, a grandchild, and a good job. High school rodeo did it for me. It gave me confidence, providing me with a path of understanding that I can do anything I want."

"What a blessing that rodeo program was for us. Reed, you can't imagine the impact it has had on our lives," Tim affirmed.

John then added, "That is the only reason I graduated from high school."

Shorty said, "You taught me the value of positive thinking. It's all in the mind. High school rodeo gave me the desire to hold on for my diploma."

"My best memories were the way you helped me to be more positive, giving me a new hold on life," Chief told me. "I was a teenager headed down the wrong road. There was a time when I didn't even want to go to school. Building that new arena, participating in those rodeo schools, being in high school rodeos, and taking Zig Ziglar's 'I Can' class all gave me a new lease on life. Without you, I probably would not have made it."

"That rodeo program was good for all of us," Kelly said. "It has made us all better people. Those memories have become the highlight of our lives."

Casey B. said, "I would not have traded that high school rodeo experience for anything. It kept a lot of kids out of trouble. Some of those kids were going down the wrong road. It created a new interest, something that got attention to do good rather than bad."

Jerry added, "That rodeo program kept a whole bunch of us in school. It gave us a purpose and made things exciting and fulfilling. It left a big imprint in my life." Suddenly, he went silent, seeming deep in thought, then said, "Without that high school rodeo program in the school, I would have been a high school dropout. I know I would have ended up in jail."

My thoughts for teachers and students: High school students today should be experiencing what the SideKicks experienced forty years ago. How much better off would students be if they could master the ability to take risks, face their fears, and learn how to deal with failure? Every student should have the opportunity to belong, to experience natural highs, and to learn how to be resilient.

Cowboy Essence is the satisfaction in knowing you do the best you are capable of becoming. The cowboy culture has long been admired for many wonderful characters: hard work. Integrity, ambition. Self-reliance, family values, confidence, honesty, loyalty, having a good relationship with the seasons of the year. And perseverance through the hard times as well as gratitude for the good times.[27]

The choices and efforts we put forth today, either as a young person or an adult who works with young people, pave the road for the rest of the journey. You can make your life wonderful. The choice is yours.

In closing, it's worth quoting Booker T. Washington again: "Where ever our lives touch yours, we help or hinder . . . wherever yours touches ours, you make us stronger or weaker. There is no mistake . . . man drags man down or man lifts man up."[28]

Your thoughts?

PROMPTINGS

Dream • Plan • Act

"*Everything is created twice, first in the mind and then in reality.*"
Robin Sharma

Dream • Plan • Act

Dream • Plan • Act

Dream • Plan • Act

Dream • Plan • Act

Dream • Plan • Act

Dream • Plan • Act

Dream • Plan • Act

Dream • Plan • Act

Dream • Plan • Act

ACKNOWLEDGMENTS

It just didn't feel right for me not to try and make a difference. It just felt wrong to take the Sidekicks' story to the grave with me, especially after my wife said on many occasions that their story should be shared. As I accepted the challenge, I felt at times that it was beyond my ability. After meeting that challenge, another feeling—to write a sequel to the SideKicks' story of lessons learned—began to haunt me.

My thanks goes beyond those being acknowledged here to many who have been contributors in one way or another to the story of the SideKicks and this sequel. Thank you. Writing a book is very much a team effort.

To Dr. Nadine Matis, thank you for coming aboard. Your willingness to share your insights throughout this book, along with writing the foreword, preface, and epilogue, is much appreciated.

To noted writer, author, and poet Rod Miller, thanks for sharing your twenty-one-year challenge with us with us.

Many thanks to Eschler Editing for their talented assistance, especially Angela Eschler, Heidi Brockbank, Michele Preisendorf, Kimberly Durtschi, Eugene Woodbury, and Chris Bigelow.

And to the many friends and family who have helped this book in innumerable ways, my deepest appreciation.

ABOUT THE AUTHORS

Reed Thomas is a native of Wales, Utah. He received his bachelors in education from Utah State University in 1966 and his master's in education from Northern Arizona University in 1972. He completed additional graduate work that led to an educational endorsement from Brigham Young University.

He taught for thirty-seven years in the public-school systems of California, Nevada, and Utah. He also taught BYU's Education Psychology 514 R, "Attitudes and Communication" at Snow College for teacher recertification.

His side interests include the raising of beef cattle and registered quarter horses, as well as team roping. At his annual "Top of the Crop" production sale, he marketed quarter horses throughout the United States and Canada. In 1999, he was selected King Cowboy by the Sanpete County Cattlemen Association. He organized and chaired the Sanpitch Cowboy Expo in celebration of the National Day of the American Cowboy. He served as cochairman of the Hub City Days Rodeo committee for several years. He gives tribute to his mentor and hero, his father, a true American Cowboy, for these past life experiences.

His civic service includes completing a term as mayor in his hometown of Wales, as a member of the Mount Pleasant City Council, and as vice president of the construction of the Contoy Indoor Arena during its first six years of development. On July 4, 2017, he and his wife, Robyn, were honored as grand marshals of the Hub City Independence Days Parade in Mount Pleasant, Utah.

Nadine Matis is a native of Ogden, Utah. She received her bachelors in education from the University of Utah, her master's of education in counseling and guidance from Brigham Young University, and her PhD in counseling psychology from Brigham Young University.

During the first five years of her employment, she worked as a counseling psychologist for the Weber County School District. She then served as the counseling therapist at the Center of Counseling and Therapeutic Services of the McKay Dee Hospital Institute for Behavioral Medicine. There she was the director of the Adolescent Inpatient Program.

For ten years, she was the counseling psychologist at the Counseling Center of Weber State University, serving as adjunct professor of psychology. During that period, she counseled students, developed curriculum for psychology classes, and taught classes. She also represented the university as a consultant, public speaker, and workshop presenter.

In 1990, she was honored as the Utah State and US Mother of the Year. Married to John A. Matis, she is the mother of four children and grandmother of eight.

She and her husband served as missionaries in 2000–2002 in the office of the Pacific Islands area presidency. She worked under the direction of the area presidency with six mission presidents to assist with the psychological and emotional problems of the missionaries serving in the area.

She continues to work with youth and adults in need of counseling.

NOTE TO READERS

Your review of my books on Amazon and/or Barnes and Noble is much appreciated.

My heart continues to sing as I see our youth experience success, even against the odds. Our most important work is not behind but ahead of us as we support our young people in moving into the next greatest generation.

If you'd like to use my books as a fund-raiser as we promote this cause, or for me to be a presenter at an assembly within your school, contact me at rthomas@reedthomas.org.

ENDNOTES

1. New York: Simon and Schuster, 1960.
2. New York: Aladdin Paperbacks, 1954.
3. Merriam-Webster, https://www.merriam-webster.com/dictionary/sixth%20sense; accessed October 15, 2018.
4. Nancy Murphy, *Whisperings of the Spirit*, Salt lake City, UT: Deseret Book Company, 2008, 33; used by permission.
5. Goodreads, accessed March 8, 2016, http://www.goodreads.com/quotes/2528-keep-away-from- people-who-try-to-belittle-your-ambitions.
6. "Booker T. Washington Quotes," Wisdom of the Wise.com, accessed March 8, 2016, http://www.wisdom-of-the-wise.com/Booker-T-Washington.htm.
7. Goodreads, https://www.goodreads.com/quotes/1333370-judge-tenderly-if-you-must-there-is-usually-a-side; accessed October 15, 2018.
8. Goodreads, https://www.goodreads.com/quotes/544579-most-folks-are-about-as-happy-as-they-make-up; accessed October 15, 2018.
9. Lois M. Collins, "Why You Want to Get Out of Your Comfort Zone—and How to Do It," *Deseret News*, July 30, 2017, P3.
10. Ibid.
11. Goodreads, https://www.goodreads.com/quotes/495741-everything-you-want-is-on-the-other-side-of-fear; accessed October 15, 2018.
12. Doug Wilks, "Study Shows Quantity Time Beats Quality Time with Teens," *Deseret News,* July 30, 2017, P12.
13. https://www.merriam-webster.com/dictionary/mentor
14. Goodreads, https://www.goodreads.com/quotes/2528-keep-away-from-people-who-try-to-belittle-your-ambitions; accessed October 15, 2018.
15. Jack Canfield, *The Success Principals, William Morrow*, Harper Collins Publishers, 2005, 212.
16. "Innovation," Wikipedia: https://en.wikipedia.org/wiki/Innovation.
17. Eric Zorn, "Without Failure, Jordan Would Be False Idol, *Chicago Tribune,* May 19, 1997, http://www.chicagotribune.com/news/ct-xpm-1997-05-19-9705190096-story.html.
18. Goodreads, https://www.goodreads.com/quotes/648499-everything-is-created-twice-first-in-the-mind-and-then; accessed October 15, 2018.
19. Carter Crocker and Earl Geurs*, Poof's Grand Adventure: The Search of Christopher Robin* (1997).

20. "The People in Pictures," *Life*, July 1993, 84.
21. Stephen R. Covey Home, accessed March 17, 2016, https://www.stephencovey.com/7habits/7habits-habit2.php.
22. Ibid.
23. Steve Densley, "Facing the 'What If' Moment in Each of Our Lives," *Daily Herald*, July 30, 2017, C4.
24. https://addicted2success.com/motivation/video-joe-rogan-be-the-hero-of-your-own-movie/
25. Goodreads, https://www.goodreads.com/quotes/407245-there-are-some-things-which-cannot-be-learned-quickly-and; accessed October 15, 2018.
26. "Rusty Bench Named Grand Marshal of Fairview Horse Parade," *The Pyramid,* July 20, 2017, 6.
27. The Constitution of the Babbitt Ranches, Article III, 2013, Horse Sale Catalog, Babbitt Ranches, Flagstaff, Arizona; used with permission.
28. "Booker T. Washington Quotes," Wisdom of the Wise.com, accessed March 8, 2016, http://www.wisdom-of-the-wise.com/Booker-T-Washington.htm.

www.ingramcontent.com/pod-product-compliance
Lightning Source LLC
Chambersburg PA
CBHW032358040426
42451CB00006B/47